BRIAN MOSES

KEEPING CLEAR OF PARADISE STREET

A SEASIDE CHILDHOOD IN THE 1950s

ILLUSTRATED BY NATHAN HUDSON

Published by
Candy Jar Books
Mackintosh House, 136 Newport Road
Cardiff, CF24 1DJ
www.candyjarbooks.co.uk

A catalogue record of this book is available
from the British Library

ISBN: 978-0-9933221-8-1

Printed and bound in the UK by
CPI Antony Rowe, Chippenham, Wiltshire, UK

Cover and illustrations: Nathan Hudson
Edited by William Rees & Shaun Russell

Oh, those were the days when you were young, Dad,
long ago before my birth,
when televisions were black and white
and dinosaurs ruled the Earth!

Brian Moses

Most of this is true, although I am primarily a poet, and a poet has poetic licence!

All characters in this book who are not family members are amalgamations of different people I knew. Some of the things that happened in the school chapters would certainly not be allowed to happen today.

In memory of my parents, Harry & Margaret.

To Vanessa —

tellin' it like it was —

Frank

Contents

— CHAPTER ONE —

This Kissing Business

I spent much of my childhood wondering how anyone could possibly enjoy kissing. It just seemed the most ridiculously unappealing, unattractive thing to do to anyone. I was very particular about what I did with my mouth. Eating, talking, whistling, spitting (when no one was looking) and yelling were OK, but I knew I didn't, knew I wouldn't ever, enjoy kissing. You could just about put up with it when your mum kissed you goodnight, or just before you went to school (but not in front of your mates, no, never in front of your mates). And even being kissed by an elderly aunt was bearable providing you turned your head and made very sure it was only your cheek she kissed. But even then the smell of perfume could almost make you gag. Perfume was supposed to make someone smell nice, but it didn't seem to work on elderly aunts. Perhaps they'd kept it too long and it was way past its sell by date (not that we had sell by dates in the 1950s). You learnt to stop breathing for a moment and put up with it, particularly if your aunt was pressing money into your hand at the same time.

At Christmas time, of course, the aunts would gang up on me, catch me under the mistletoe and stand there, lips puckered up, expecting me to run into their embrace. No way – I was good at dodging outstretched arms.

You'd see couples kissing on the TV, of course, but I just didn't get it. Why on earth would you want to sucker your mouth, limpet-like, onto someone else's mouth and hold it there? Why would you want to trade your saliva with somebody else's? I'd read somewhere that we all have huge numbers of germs in our saliva, so why risk someone else's germs playing tag with mine? It just didn't make any sense. Why do it? Why take that risk?

There had to be some reason why billions of people all over the world went at it so enthusiastically. From quick pecks on the cheek, to mouth-on-mouth squelches, to sliding kisses that left their trail across the face, it was all a big mystery to me. And what if the person you kissed had a cold? What if he or she sneezed as you were about to kiss and your face was sprayed with flying snot? Who in their right mind would want that?

It was all very confusing. And it became even more puzzling when in my final year at primary school I began to think that kissing Brenda Miller just might actually be enjoyable!

Of all the girls in my class, Brenda was the one who disturbed the boys. She was an absolute stunner, with the sort of smile that could melt a boy's frozen heart. All the boys fell for her while at the same time pretending that they hadn't.

Brenda knew the effect she was having. She would ask a favour and the boys would form a queue to grant it. Although we'd never have admitted it, we dreamt of Brenda, of marrying her and setting up home together. Any boy in that year would have signed, sealed and delivered his own future at the feet of Brenda Miller if she'd only asked him to. I never really knew where I stood in any rankings she gave to the boys. Was I third or thirty-third in her affections? We couldn't tell. Brenda treated everyone the same.

One day it was raining hard and I saw the opportunity to get myself noticed. I'd read how Sir Walter Raleigh, a Tudor nobleman, had laid his cloak over a puddle so that

Queen Elizabeth I could keep from getting her feet wet. Puddles in the playground meant that I could do the same for Brenda.

At home time I made sure I was out in the yard early, and lingered by the doors until I heard Brenda coming. This was my chance. I was Sir Walter. My coat was in my hand, a puddle at my feet, and as Brenda emerged with her friends I swept my coat down before her. Queen Elizabeth probably smiled at such a gracious act, but Brenda just laughed. 'You'll be in deep trouble with your mum,' she said, and walked off giggling with her mates.

I was amazed. I was devastated. My grand and selfless act had been dismissed in a moment. Maybe I'd hoped she would be so impressed that she'd fling her arms around my neck and let me discover what I was missing about kissing. Maybe I'd thought that my efforts would boost me several places in her affections. In the end I reasoned that she wasn't mature enough to appreciate what I'd done for her. But she was right in one respect; I did get into huge trouble with my mum.

— CHAPTER TWO —

Mustn't Grumble

I was forever getting into some sort of trouble with my mum and dad. Often it was because I failed to listen to something they were telling me, intent instead on following some concern of my own. Whenever my dad started a sentence with, 'When I was a boy,' it was the cue for me to switch off and think of something else. This happened a lot; he loved to talk about his childhood.

And now I'm writing a whole book about when I was

a boy, and hoping you won't switch off before I get a chance to tell you about *my* childhood.

When I was a boy we only had black and white television, and that only had two channels: BBC and ITV. If we wanted to change the channel, we had to get up out of our seats, as there were no remotes. We had no computers, no Internet, no mobile phones, no Playstations, no Xboxes, no X Factor, no DVDs, no iPods, no shopping centres, no pizzas, no MacDonalds...

How did we survive?

My childhood was straight out of *The Dangerous Book for Boys*. I did some risky things and I sometimes wonder how I survived! I've tried to recall a lot of the things in this book, but I can't be certain in the early years how much I actually remember.

Sometimes the things I remember are real memories, and other times I'm convinced that my ideas about my childhood come from the grainy black and white photographs that filled my parents' albums.

There was the time we moved house – not very far, just across the road and down the hill a little bit. The house was newly constructed, one of three that had been built to replace others that had been bombed in the war. I remember, or think I remember, moving day. We didn't need a van, just a bit of man power provided by Dad, his brother and their friend so that the furniture could be shifted. I helped too, crossing the road swinging a saucepan in each hand. I was only two years old... so do I actually remember this or is it something I'd been told about?

Then there was the street party to celebrate Queen Elizabeth II becoming Queen. I was three years old. Can I really remember the long line of tables down the centre of our street? Everyone bringing out tables from their houses, covering them with table cloths and piling on all kinds of food prepared by everyone in the street? My mum making her party piece, homemade sausage rolls? Or is it that I can picture the photograph of me stuffing my face with jelly and cake?

Can I really remember those first television programmes, with doggy hero Rin Tin Tin or Champion the Wonder Horse or Davy Crockett, King of the Wild Frontier? (Joke: Did you know that Davy Crockett had three ears? A left ear, a right ear and a wild frontier!)

I suppose I'll never know for sure. I'll do my best to remember what I can, and whether everything happened exactly as I tell it, well, you'll just have to take my word for it, and hopefully I'll be able to show you something of what childhood was like when I was a boy.

My great-grandad was the lighthouse keeper at Dungeness Lighthouse in Kent. There's a photograph of him and my great-grandma hanging on the curving wall of the lighthouse, and I have a copy of that photograph hanging on the wall in my house too. (That's not immediately relevant to this story, but I thought I'd start with something that might impress you!)

My dad was born in Ramsgate in 1911. His parents, Pop and Nellie, owned a furniture store in the town. He was one of five children, including brothers Jack and George and sisters Doris and Nellie. Dad would tell me stories of his childhood: how he had a good voice and sang solo for his school.

My mum was born in London. Her father left home soon after she was born, leaving his wife, Annie, to look after her. They moved to Ramsgate when my mum was three. Annie worked as a cleaner to try and make some money, but they were never very well off. My mum passed the exam to go to the town's grammar school, but Annie couldn't afford to pay for the uniform, so she attended St George's secondary modern. This was the same school my dad went to, but they wouldn't have met there as my mum was eight years younger than my dad.

When they did meet, my dad wasn't very impressed as Mum was the 'baby' of the group that he went around with. But over time they realised that there was some kind of attraction between them. My mum was working in a draper's shop, selling all kinds of fabrics, while my dad worked in his parents' furniture store along with his brother Jack.

When the Second World War broke out in 1939, my

mum joined the WRENS (the Women's Royal Naval Service) and was based in Ramsgate throughout the war. My dad wanted to join the army, but his father wouldn't let him leave the family business. Dad was short-sighted, and it was doubtful whether he would have passed the medical anyway. He worked in the shop until 1941, when the army needed more men and Dad was conscripted (told that he would have to join up). His short-sightedness was ignored, but he wasn't allowed to fight in the front lines. Instead he was offered a post in the RAMC, the Royal Army Medical Corps.

He did his basic training and, before he left to go overseas, asked my mum to marry him. She said yes, but neither of them knew that it would be almost five more years before they could actually get married. Dad was sent to North Africa where the Germans were being fought in the desert. After the war he would never talk about what he actually did as a male nurse, but I know that he helped ease the suffering of wounded soldiers from both sides. Sometimes though, he'd tell me about strange or amusing things that happened like trying to shower with a bucket of water or removing scorpions from inside his army boots. From North Africa he went to Italy, where, despite the war, he managed to do quite a lot of sightseeing in cities like Naples, Rome and Florence.

All the time they were apart my parents wrote to each other and talked of the day the war would be over and they would be back together. They were finally married in June 1946, and I was born in June 1950.

Soon after I was born my dad was diagnosed with the illness diabetes. He had to give himself injections of something called insulin twice a day to help control the disease. Sometimes, however, at the end of a day when Dad had been working hard and was cycling home for tea, he would feel unwell and know that if he didn't get home soon he might collapse.

If he was late getting home, Mum would often send me to see if he was in sight. I'd run to the top of the hill and wait till he cycled into our street, then I'd race him down to the gate. He'd park his bicycle in our side entrance, tug the clips from his trousers and come in through the back door.

Mum could tell immediately if there was something wrong. He'd answer questions, vague and bemused, and we'd find it hard to make out what he was saying. His face would be white and Mum would push food into his mouth to try and stop the diabetic attack.

As he ate, the colour would return to his face. I'd realise that my eyes were wet and I'd blink the tea table back into focus. He'd smile at me and hold out his hand. 'Sorry, son' he'd say. Often he'd pull out of his pocket a toy soldier or a model car, something he'd probably bought weeks ago and kept ready in case he needed it, something to help show me that my dad wasn't so strange after all.

It was a huge worry though, especially to my mum. There were two occasions when he was too far gone for her to rescue him. He'd collapsed at the tea table dragging the table cloth and all the tea things with him. We had no phone in the house and I was sent racing to the corner shop to ask them to phone for an ambulance. He spent a couple of nights in hospital while they sorted out the diabetes and made sure he was fit again.

Whether we were at home or if we were out, we had to make sure that Dad got his meals on time. Any delay could trigger 'one of his turns.' As a kid I think I was able to escape from the worry, to put it to one side and carry on with my life and my interests, but Mum lived with it every hour of every day, and she suffered with her nerves greatly because of it.

Despite his illness, my dad would always be there for me, making things, taking us on the train for day visits to London, playing games in the park and generally trying hard to make sure that the dad I had wasn't too different from other kids' dads.

All this time he was still working in his parents' furniture shop. He would often return home with minor injuries There were often gashes on his head from where he'd stood up too quickly from laying floor covering and hit his head on a shelf. These always seemed to be in the places where his hair didn't grow, and Mum would tell him he should be more careful. Or he'd blacken a nail, usually one of his thumb nails, hammering down carpet tacks and missing and hitting his thumb instead. I'd notice the black patch against the white of the half-moon in his nail, and watch the blackness shift over the weeks until, months later, it cleared his nail and disappeared.

Mercifully, his injuries were generally less dramatic, like the times he'd cut himself shaving and turn up at the breakfast table with white patches of toilet paper clinging to his skin.

In 1962 my dad bought a greenhouse. It came by post in separate pieces and he jigsawed it together. I tried to help but I was a duff apprentice. The framework shook when I handled it. 'Let me do it,' Dad said, 'you're far too cackhanded.' It was a favourite word of his, 'cackhanded', and it wasn't the first time he'd called me it. Dad carried on by himself and in no time at all the framework was bolted and firm. He then cut the glass to fit the panels. I kept well clear, knowing if I touched anything it would break. I played safe and mixed the putty that Dad used to fix the glass to the frame.

Mum said Dad had green fingers. Our neighbours said so too. I looked each day for evidence that Dad was slowly changing into an alien from outer space, first his fingers, then his hands, arms, legs and so on. Fortunately, he never did. But he was good with gardening and he grew fantastic vegetables.

One of the things that my dad was always on the lookout for was horse poo! He knew that vegetables grew better with fertilizer, and he knew that horse poo was great fertilizer. Even better, it was free. Most weekends the 'rag-and-bone' man would come down our street with his horse and cart, hunting for household items that were being thrown away, particularly scrap metal, which he could sell somewhere. We would hear him calling out 'rag and bone' as he came down the hill, and this would put Dad on high alert. He'd have his bucket ready, and if he struck lucky he'd be hurrying up the hill to lay claim to what the horse had left behind. I wouldn't go anywhere near it, and I found his activities a huge source of embarrassment. Nobody else's dad went running after horse poo! Once the bucket had been brought back, he would dig a trench and tip in its contents, before planting his lettuces or cabbages in the stinky stuff and covering it with soil. It did worry me that we were eating vegetables that had grown in horse manure, but they grew so well and tasted so good that I reasoned my dad must have known what he was doing after all.

Dad seemed to know a huge amount of people in Ramsgate, and whenever we met someone he knew and they asked how he was, he'd answer, 'Mustn't grumble.' Years later I bought an old postcard of Ramsgate with the message on the back, 'Had a storm yesterday but never mind, mustn't grumble.' It took me back, and I wondered what else Dad might have applied it to: the bike's got a puncture, the dog's left home, the house has fallen down – still, mustn't grumble!

My mum, meanwhile, had a saying for every occasion. If I asked for something expensive from the toy shop window, she'd come back at me with, 'Money doesn't grow on trees,' or 'What do you think I am, made of money?' If she wasn't feeling quite right, she'd say, 'I'm feeling anyhow today.' At night she'd tell me it was time to go 'Up the wooden hill to Bedfordshire,' where I should be ready to 'Sink into the arms of the Sandman.' If she asked me a question and I didn't reply, she'd say, 'What's the matter? Cat got your tongue?' If I pulled a face she'd warn, 'The wind will change and leave you stuck.' And if I complained about how hard my homework was, she'd say, 'Can't do was made to do.' or 'Take the 't' off of can't and you can.' And that's just a few of them!

For Mum, as for millions of other women, Monday was always wash day. We had no washing machine, so everything was washed in the sink by hand. Washing took up most of the day, and once everything was washed it had to be hung on the line to dry (if the weather was fine) or else put through a mangle to help squeeze it dry. A mangle consisted of two heavy rollers in a frame, connected by cogs. Turning a handle set the rollers moving, which pulled the wet washing between them so that the water was squeezed out. I was fascinated by the machine and liked to play with it when it wasn't in use. My mum would always warn me about it because she knew of a young girl whose fingers were squashed between the rollers. 'Never tangle with a mangle,' was the rhythmic warning she'd give me.

Dad and I always found it amusing when, if we were walking in the countryside or watching fields from a railway carriage window, my mum would suddenly say, 'It'll rain later.' My mum thought that if cows were huddled together in a field, then that was a sign that rain would soon fall. If they were well spaced out and chewing grass, then there were no weather worries. Is there any truth in that? Beats me!

It was always Dad's job to take me for a haircut, and we visited the barbers where he had been going since he was a boy. I always thought that, as there wasn't much hair left on his head, Dad should have had a special discount, but whatever there was needed cutting, or so he said, and so he still paid the same price as everyone else. I hated the barbers. First we'd have to wait in a queue while others had their hair cut. And when our turn came round, the barber, Mr Dawes, would joke with me, suggesting that he do exotic things with my hair. Dad would peer around from behind his paper and say, 'Just the usual for the boy, please.' I'd then be given my short back and sides. On one occasion, when I was very young and probably wriggling around in the chair, Mr Dawes caught my ear with his scissors and it bled a bit. I was always terrified that he'd misjudge things again and that next time the whole ear might be severed. I hated my ears because they were large and stuck up from my head like jug handles, but at least they were a matching pair. I knew I would have looked even worse with just one!

— CHAPTER THREE —

A 'Chips With Everything' Sort Of Place

I grew up in Ramsgate, a seaside town on the coast of north Kent and part of the Isle of Thanet, which is an island only by name. It was a proper island in Roman times, but over the years the channel between Thanet and the rest of Kent filled up with sand and mud till all that remained was a river. The river is called the Wantsum, and we always joked as kids that this was because it wanted some more water!

Ramsgate was a seaside town in the days before everyone started jetting off to Spain or Portugal. It was a 'kiss-me-quick', chips with everything, bucket-and-spade sort of place, and everyone who holidayed in Ramsgate always wanted to sit on the Sands.

One of my earliest memories is of playing on the Sands, but, again, I'm not sure if I actually remember this, or if it's from a photograph in the family album. All I know is that I wasn't fashionably dressed; the swimsuit I was wearing was hideous, and the sun hat was even worse!

There are photos too of sandcastles that my dad and I built, with channels running down to the sea so that water could reach our carefully constructed moat. Tiny flags flapped on top of sand pies that we emptied out of buckets. The sand, of course, had to be the right texture – not too dry, not too sloppy – so that when the bucket was upended, a perfect tower of sand appeared.

Leaving the beach to go home was sad, and there was always a decision to be made about whether to leave the sandcastle for others to play with, or whether to jump on it and stamp it flat. I don't think I was too good with the idea of sharing things at that age, so I liked to believe I was a giant whose big feet could destroy buildings.

From an early age I always liked to ride the beach donkeys. They were led along in teams of four, their names written on straps above their eyes: Neddy, Noddy,

Dolly and Joe. When I was small, my dad would walk beside me, his hand on my back to steady me as I rode along. Later on it was fun to pretend that the donkeys were horses and that I was a cowboy riding the desert trail. All day, beneath the summer sun, they would be guided along the beach, carrying young children or teenagers eating candyfloss, sometimes with parents too, or the occasional stout gran or grandad bumping along and laughing for the camera.

As I got older I felt sorry for the donkeys; it couldn't have been much of a life. Sometimes we'd see them in the morning being led through the busy streets from their field at the back of the town, shaggy creatures jammed at the traffic lights till the cars unscrambled themselves and a crack of command shifted the team. In the evening we'd see them again, returning to the field for a well-earned night's rest, till it all started up once more, the trekking and the turning over and over again.

Further along the beach were the giant swingboats, which were great fun to ride in, and the Punch and Judy Show. I was never that captivated by Mr Punch hitting everyone with a big stick, but I did enjoy seeing him caught between the jaws of the crocodile.

On the promenade by the Sands there were stalls that sold food that came from the sea. There were shellfish such as cockles, winkles, mussels and whelks, and I knew there was nothing that would make me eat them. I knew where they were found. The ones that grew to the biggest size were collected from close to the sewage pipes that ran out from the town, across the beach and into the sea. If something supposedly edible had been feeding on what came out of one of the town's sewage pipes, then I surely didn't want to know. That wasn't for me.

The 'grockles' didn't seem to mind. 'Grockles' was a term that originated in the West Country – Cornwall and Devon – and described the holidaymakers who filled up seaside towns in the summer months. There would often be fights between the local children and those who came on holiday with their parents. We would make unpleasant remarks about them as they strolled the prom in the evening before disappearing into their bed and breakfast accommodation.

Even worse than the shellfish were the jellied eels. I knew about eels. I'd caught them when fishing from the pier, slimy squirmy creatures that tied your tackle into knots as you tried to unhook them. Jellied eels were eels that had been chopped into pieces and then boiled in water and vinegar. The jelly forms as the eels are cooked. I'd look at the tiny plates of jellied eels and know that there was no way I'd be able to slide these rubbery looking things into my insides, no way I could slip that vinegary tasting stuff past my lips. And yet those who came on holiday forked them up with great delight.

For a special treat, we would travel on the train to

Margate, where we would enjoy the main attraction on Margate seafront: a funfair called Dreamland.

Most times we went there in the evening, and as we entered we would see lights in the trees and pass by shops and stalls selling all kinds of joke shop goods, from false teeth to evil-looking rubbery masks. These were always a great attraction to me, and I'd have to be discouraged from spending my pocket money on a whoopee cushion or a tin of Dr Foster's Fabulous Fart Powder.

One of my favourite activities there and, the first one we usually visited, was Hook a Duck. I always liked it because you were guaranteed a prize every time. You'd be given a 'fishing rod' with a hook on the end of the line, and this would need to be manoeuvred through a metal ring on the duck's back so you could lift it out of the water on which it was floating. The ducks had numbers on their bases which you couldn't see until they were lifted up. These numbers corresponded to prizes on the shelves behind. Most of the time the prizes would be disappointing, but occasionally someone would win a huge stuffed bear or a model car.

We loved the tubs too. This was a ride on water in a round tub that could hold up to four people. The tub would spin round and then be drawn up a series of rollers into a network of caves decorated with scenes from fairytales and pantomimes. My mum and dad would enjoy quietly looking around them, but in other tubs there were always people hooting and hollering to hear the echo on their voices.

When I was tiny my favourite ride was a small train that went round and round on a track. On this I could pretend I was a proper engine driver, holding the wheel with one hand and ringing a bell with the other. Fortunately I didn't get dizzy on this activity like I did on roundabouts. I longed to ride the ornate galloping horses known as 'gallopers', but they spun round so fast that my parents knew that I'd be sick when the ride stopped, particularly if I'd just eaten candyfloss.

There was always a big decision halfway through the evening: should I have candyfloss or a toffee apple? Whatever I chose, we would go and sit somewhere quietly to eat it, while my dad and mum had an ice cream.

Then my mum would insist that I did nothing too active for half an hour or so, just in case!

The one thing I had to pester my parents to take me to was the Dreamland Flea Circus. I only got my way once. We entered a tiny tent and gathered round a miniature circus ring to watch a strange activity that I'd only seen once before on a television programme called *Michael Bentine's Potty Time*. There was glass in front of us that magnified the activities, and we watched as fleas (the ones that humans get, apparently, as animal ones are too large!) were harnessed to tiny carts, which they pulled along behind them. Others would ride miniature bicycles or walk on a tightrope. We couldn't actually see the fleas, just the cart moving and the bicycles wobbling and the tightrope swaying. My dad claimed it was all done with thin wires and puffs of air to make you believe you'd seen the fleas. But I wasn't sure. I'm still not sure today!

There was also something called The Sphinx, a smaller version of the Egyptian original, which was really part house of fun and part spooky mansion. I don't remember much about it apart from distorting mirrors that made you look thin one minute and fat the next. It was quite dark inside, and everyone would gather round the entrance to listen to the girls scream as a blast of compressed air blew up their skirts as they went inside.

The helter skelter was fun – I loved whizzing down the slide and round the curves on the coconut matting. The dodgems too were a must, although my dad hated me driving because all I seemed to do was crash into everyone else. I'm sure he suffered from whiplash on a couple of occasions, although he was very good at hiding it from me.

Dreamland also had (and still has) the oldest timber scenic railway in the UK. I was never allowed on as my mum was worried about its safety. To be honest, I was secretly pleased, as I was sure if I were my motion sickness would kick in, and when the ride came to a halt, I would be left both green in the face and staggering about. But I loved to stand beneath it as the cars passed overhead. There would be such a noise as they rattled by, and this would mix in with the screams and shouts of the riders.

We loved the rides, but we also loved the amusement arcades, which gobbled our piles of pennies at an amazing rate. Best were the Roll a Penny machines, where you lined up your coin on a slope then let it slide into the machine, where it rolled for a bit before toppling sideways. If the penny landed completely between any of the white and black lines painted inside, you won a few more pennies as a prize. You could walk away with these and feel you'd beaten the system, but no one ever did. The pennies went back into the machines until they'd all gone.

On one occasion, when I'd started going to Dreamland with my mates, I was leaning on the game a little too hard, trying to cheat the system and influence the rolling of my penny. Suddenly I felt a hand grip my shoulder. I looked up into the face of one of the arcade attendants, who growled at me and dragged me to meet the manager in his office. I stood there while he lectured me, and too frightened to give a false name and address, I rattled off my details while he wrote them down in a book. He told me that this was a warning, and that if he found me trying to cheat again, he'd call the police. Then he steered me out of his room and through the arcade to the street. Think of it as a friendly warning, he told me, sending me on my way with a shove from his boot. I could have told my dad that he'd assaulted me, because that's what it was, but I didn't. And the manager knew I wouldn't too.

But an evening in Dreamland with my parents generally ended on a brighter note. Before we set off home, Dad would buy chips. We would stand to eat these while watching the firework display that closed the evening's activities. Today, of course, we're all used to huge displays at New Year and on special occasions, but in the 1950s and early 1960s we were easily impressed.

Living by the sea, of course, it was recommended that we all learnt to swim, just in case of accidents.

My dad had taught me to ride a bike, so it should be simple for me to learn to swim. Or so he thought. He'd do it in the same way – he'd hold on till I picked up speed then let me go. But whereas with the bike I'd managed to pedal furiously and somehow keep going, swimming didn't seem to work the same way.

I'd flail my arms around and kick out my legs, but I never seemed to get anywhere, till finally my dad was so exasperated that he let go. At that point I simply sank to the bottom then came up spluttering, spitting out sea water.

'One day, you'll manage it,' he'd say. But I knew I wouldn't. I thought of some of my mum's favourite sayings: 'That'll happen when the cows come home,' or 'when my ship comes in.' Or, 'Yes, and pigs might fly.' I felt that way about swimming. When pigs were sighted flying in formation over Ramsgate, that would be the time I'd manage a stroke or two.

My swimming teacher, Mr Mankelow, knew nothing about flying pigs. His proud boast was that everyone learnt to swim in his class, and he wouldn't allow me to be an exception. He was determined that I should swim by the time I left primary school. So once a week in my last summer term of primary school, he would march us all to the local swimming pool. It seemed that every time we were stood on the lip of this cavernous open air pool, the temperature would drop and the wind would rise, and the last place any of us wanted to be was shivering by the side.

I was very thin. 'Slim', my mother preferred, or 'wiry'. When I lay back and attempted to float, I immediately sank to the bottom. There was nothing to support me, nothing to help me float. It was hopeless. *I* was hopeless according to Mr Mankelow, but he wouldn't give up.

He'd get us into the pool and we would have to hold onto the edge while flapping our feet. Then, slowly, he'd walk along the poolside, his feet creeping closer to our hands. 'Come on, boy, you're not even trying,' he'd yell at one of us, then bring his foot down on the unlucky boy's fingers. There'd be a howl and a great thrashing about in the water as the victim let go of the side.

Mr Makelow's thinking was that the shock of finding yourself adrift in the water would force you to swim, and, indeed, on one or two occasions, this probably happened. But with me it was quite the reverse. I was very good at thrashing about, but none of my limbs ever seemed to move in any kind of co-ordinated way, and cast off from the poolside I would quickly sink to the bottom taking in great gobfulls of pool water as I went.

And this – swallowing the pool water – worried me perhaps even more than the stamp of Mr Mankelow's boot. I knew how many kids used to pee in that pool. There was chlorine in the water to kill germs, but I couldn't get away from the idea that as I sunk, inevitably, to the bottom, I'd be swallowing some unidentified boy's pee. How long would it take, I used to wonder, before it was a pool of pee and not water? It was a question that could be turned into one of those mind-twisting problems that they were so fond of giving us in maths: A pool measures sixty feet by thirty feet, and holds x amount of water. Water leaks from the pool at a rate of twenty gallons a day, but small boys pee back ten gallons a day. How long will it be before the pool is empty? Well, something like that.

My cousin David was a very strong swimmer. Not only that, he was a champion diver as well. Not for him the lower diving boards – he'd climb to the highest level.

We'd go to watch him sometimes and see him standing on the lip of the board, ready to hurl himself into the abyss. He would manage to twist and turn in the air too, before slicing into the water. How I longed to be confident in the pool like David.

I knew what would happen if I ever tried anything like that. Get it wrong and you'd hit the water with a *slap*. There was a rumour that one lad hit the water so hard that his stomach split and his guts fell out. That would be me. By the time I left Primary School I still hadn't learnt to swim. It was a bad year, according to Mr Mankelow, as there were three of us who, whenever his boot came down, would still end up floundering at the bottom of the pool. We destroyed his perfect success rate, but I felt he'd had it coming. Years later, when I was a teacher myself, and still a non-swimmer, I remembered Mr Mankelow's methods and determined that however I taught swimming, or tried to teach swimming, it would be through consideration and encouragement.

CHAPTER FOUR

Going To See A Man About A Dog

Whenever my dad didn't want me to know where he was going, he'd always say, 'I'm going to see a man about a dog.' What dog? Why would he go and see a man about a dog? I wanted a dog, but he never came back with one. My dad used to see a lot of men about a lot of dogs, but one night I asked my mum where my dad had gone, and she told me that this time he really had gone to see a man about a dog. He brought the dog home too, although it was so late by the time he got back that I was in bed and, despite struggling to stay awake, had fallen fast asleep.

When I woke in the morning, I rushed downstairs to be greeted by a small black puppy teetering about in our living room. His tail was wagging so furiously it was as if I were the only person in the whole world that he wanted to see. I scooped him up into my arms and held him tightly.

We called him Chum, my chum, my pal, this small black dog with white on his paws and chest, and I knew from that moment we were made for each other. 'He's a cross,' my dad said. 'A mongrel – part spaniel and part labrador.' I didn't care what he was; he was my dog, a dog I'd longed for, and that was all that mattered.

He'd come from some relatives of ours who lived about an hour away by train. The journey had proved too much for Chum. He'd been lying on Dad's lap and suddenly Dad had felt a warm, wet sensation spreading over his legs and realised that the puppy had peed on him. It must have been quite embarrassing for Dad, having to walk home from the station with wet trousers, and he must have been thankful that it was dark.

I was disappointed that first morning. I wanted to play and play with Chum, but he was only a six-week-old puppy and still needed a lot of sleep to help build his strength up. So when he crawled into his basket and fell asleep, I reluctantly learnt to leave him be and wait for the next time he woke so that we could chase each other again.

It was a Friday night when Chum arrived, and I had the whole weekend to spend with him. But Monday morning was a real wrench. I had to leave him behind and go to school. All day I thought about my dog. I can't have got any work done. At the end of the day I zoomed out of the classroom and discovered my mum waiting at the school gates. She had a basket with her, and a little black head was peering out from beneath a cloth. She'd known how much I'd wanted my friends to meet Chum, and so she'd carried him to school. Everyone crowded round, wanting to stroke him, and of course he just loved all the attention.

Training a small dog to live with a family isn't easy. Chum was always in trouble for chewing on the table legs, attacking cushions or leaving puddles on the floor; Mum was forever mopping up behind him. If Dad found evidence of his misbehaviour first, Chum would be sent out into the garden and made to stay there. We'd hear Chum's sad whining outside the door as he waited to be let back inside. Neither Mum nor I could stand to listen to his cries, and he'd be in again in no time, only to be thrown out again by Dad when he discovered what we'd done. Dad wasn't cruel – he rightly knew that you needed to be firm with a dog when training it, something that

I've never been able to do.

As Chum grew, he started to play his part in the age old war of dogs against cats. If Chum met a cat on his daily walks, his hackles would rise all along his back, he would bark aggressively and pull like mad to reach his prey. Most cats, realising that Chum was on a lead and couldn't actually get to them, would show huge indifference to him. They would get up slowly, stretch, offer him a withering look and then saunter off in another direction. This infuriated Chum even more. On the occasions when Chum was off the lead and we met a cat, a wild chase would ensue until either the cat leapt up onto a fence or through a gap in a hedge that was far too small for Chum to follow.

There was one time, however, when Chum certainly came off best. He discovered a cat sleeping on a pile of cut grass in the far corner of our garden, under a lilac tree. He raced towards it in his usual aggressive fashion, but instead of jumping over the fence, this cat stayed where it was. It looked ready to attack, hissing and arching its back.

Chum applied the brakes a foot or so from the cat, and they stood there eyeballing each other for a minute or two. I watched with interest, unsure how this standoff would be resolved. Then, suddenly, Chum turned, lifted his leg and directed a stream of pee at the cat.

I couldn't believe what I was seeing. If I'd have been

him, would I have dared expose my private parts to possible injury from a cat's claws?

I could only guess that Chum understood that a cat's natural aversion to water of any kind would see him OK. And water was something he could supply in great abundance. Whatever it was that went through his doggy brain, it had the desired effect. The cat fled, wet and humiliated. Chum turned towards me with a satisfied look on his face. He may not have won the war, but he'd developed a brilliant new tactic.

When Chum was older, maybe around nine or ten, a cat moved in next door to us, a black and white one called Whiskey. For some strange reason, Chum didn't chase Whiskey. Our neighbours were out working for most of the day, and so Whiskey started calling round our house. My mum took pity on him, fed him all kinds of titbits, and he called round even more. I have no idea why Chum put up with seeing Whiskey in our kitchen, but Whiskey showed no fear of Chum and would slide up to him and rub himself against Chum's legs. If Chum was asleep in his basket, Whiskey would often climb in beside him and both would snooze quite comfortably together. We never understood why Chum called a truce in his war with cats to allow this one to become his friend, but he did.

Honey, the dog we have today, would be horrified to think that any dog would allow a cat to get that close to him, but Chum didn't seem to mind. Maybe he liked the extra warmth that the cat gave as she stretched out along his belly.

All his life Chum, like many dogs, hated loud noises. We dreaded Bonfire Night. As soon as he heard the first fireworks, Chum would be shivering for the rest of the evening. We always put the television on and turned up the volume to try to hide the noise, but with his extra-sensitive ears, it didn't matter how much comfort we gave him, how long we sat with him or how many reassuring words we spoke: he couldn't be calmed. Sometimes he would crawl under the table and lie there shaking, or he'd squeeze himself behind the settee. Once he did that, we left him alone, as he seemed happier to be somewhere closed in.

He behaved in a similar way when he heard the lifeboat signals. These were three very loud bangs which let the lifeboat crew know that they were needed down at the harbour to man the lifeboat. If Chum could have put his paws over his ears, he would surely have done so.

Chum hated thunder too. He seemed to know when a storm was near and would prowl restlessly from room to room. When the first claps of thunder sounded, his desire was to get up somewhere high. We never understood why. He'd climb onto a chair or onto the settee and bury his head under as many cushions as he could find. On one occasion, the table was laid for tea, and Dad, Mum and I were sitting down about to begin when we heard an enormous clap of thunder. The next thing we knew, Chum had launched himself into the air and landed in the middle of the table, scattering tea things everywhere. I remember that being one of the rare occasions I heard my dad swear, but nobody could blame him as the very hot contents of his tea cup had fountained into his lap.

Like most dogs Chum was happiest on his twice-daily walks. A dog's sense of smell is many, many times more powerful than a human's, and Chum mapped the entire neighbourhood with his nose. Each day he was keen to find out what other dogs had visited his patch, and to mark his territory once more. The longest walks we went on were on Sunday afternoons, when Dad liked to 'walk off his dinner'. Problem was that Mum and I had to go too. The Sunday afternoon walk was a tradition of my childhood. One walk was to Pegwell to see the fish pond in someone's front garden. If that doesn't sound exciting to you, then know that it certainly wasn't top of the excitement charts for me either. The only consolation was that we would stop off at the shop in the village to buy ice creams. Chum would bounce and circle our heels, begging us to let him have some.

Another walk was to a local farm where we might spot cows and horses. I liked to feed them with grass when I was young, but the novelty soon wore off and it became just another boring afternoon. One Sunday, however, Chum decided to liven things up a bit. We were walking through a field pongy with animal droppings, Chum some way ahead. We watched as he stopped to investigate something on the ground. By the time we realised what he was thinking, it was too late. He had rolled in a wet patch of farmyard manure, coating himself with something that looked like it had been shovelled out of a pig sty. He looked really funny and was wearing his I-don't-know-what-I've-just-rolled-in-but-wow-do-I-smell-good look. But Dad didn't seem to see the funny side. The smell from the manure was dreadful, ten out of ten for awfulness, although Chum seemed to think it was the highest quality perfume. Dad put Chum on the lead so he couldn't repeat the pleasure, and Mum and I walked ahead all the way back.

We cut the walk short and headed back home, where we took down the old tin bath from the fence and filled it with warm soapy water. Chum was eyeing up the bath, and we could tell he was wondering if his brief moment of pleasure had been worth it. He hated baths. He pulled back on his lead as far away from the bath as he could get.

Usually he would be lifted up and placed in the water, but Dad was worried about getting muck on his clothes. Finally, dressed in his old gardening mac, he managed to push Chum towards the bath and get his front paws in the water. But while Dad was trying to get the rest of him in, Chum twisted free and sprinted off down the garden.

It took a while till he could be cornered and captured again, and this time Mum held tight to his lead while Dad got all of him in the bath. Chum looked very sorry for himself. We needed a huge amount of soap and a lot of hard scrubbing to clean him up. Then he was doused with buckets of water to wash off the soap and finally allowed to go free.

He leapt out of the bath, ran towards us and shook himself vigorously.

If dogs can smile, then I know there was a smile on his face as he sent us running to avoid the spray. Later on I wrote about the incident in one of my poems for younger children, ending with the line, 'Our dog had a bath... and then gave us a shower.'

We kept other pets too. One day my dad was given a rabbit and brought it home in a cardboard box. After tea he set about making a hutch for it. I tried to pick up the rabbit but it bit me. We kept it for several months, but it was impossible to tame it. Mum reckoned it was wild. I thought that all our efforts to tame it seemed to make it wilder than it was in the first place. Finally one morning it escaped from the hutch and disappeared for several days. The next time we saw it was in our garden, enjoying Dad's lettuces. Dad chased it away and it was never seen again.

We also had a guinea pig that was very shy and

extremely difficult to pick up. It would skitter about all over the place, and a barrier had to be built in its hutch so it could be contained in one place and then caught.

My Uncle Jack and Aunt Olive gave us a tortoise. They had three: two males and a female. The two males didn't get on together, and so one of them came to us. We named him Tommy. Tortoises, of course, are not terribly exciting as pets. For a start, a tortoise is a half-year pet. It's around and about in summer, and then at the first hint of a temperature drop in autumn, it starts looking for somewhere to hibernate. We'd find ours beneath a pile of leaves or attempting to push his way beneath our shed. At that point Dad would pick him up and place him inside the shed in a box filled with straw. There he'd stay until spring, when the temperature rose once more. Dad would check on him throughout the winter to make sure he was OK, but apart from that nothing else was needed.

Once Tommy tried to hibernate beneath the bonfire we'd built for Bonfire Night. We looked everywhere for him, and it was only a matter of hours before we were due to light the fire that someone suggested we check it. Fortunately he was pulled out and stuck in his box before we all discovered what roasted tortoise smelt like!

One sunny day in spring, Tommy would wake up and escape from his box through an exit that Dad had cut in the side. We'd find him patrolling the shed looking for a way out. Before we let him roam the garden again, we would rub olive oil into his legs and what bits of his body we could reach, to help him move more easily after such a long sleep. For his first meal of the year he would be presented with lettuce leaves and tomato slices. His scaly jaws always looked a little stiff as he attempted to eat what was on offer.

Tortoise's jaws are stained with the colour of whatever they've just eaten. This was always a giveaway when Tommy had feasted on Dad's vegetable patch. It wasn't quite so bad when the plants had grown a little – they could stand a bit of pruning – but on one occasion Tommy discovered a row of peas that had just raised their heads through the earth. We were out at the time, and on our return Dad discovered that he'd chomped every one.

On occasions like this (they weren't uncommon – that tortoise really did have a huge appetite for young green plants) Dad would pick Tommy up and carry him down to the part of our garden nearest the house. This was concreted over, and the only way out was up two steps which led to the rest of the garden. It was really a prison exercise yard as far as Tommy was concerned. Before long he'd be prowling around it, surveying the steps, his tiny brain assessing whether he could climb them.

I'd never considered tortoises to be mountaineers, but Tommy could have made an attempt on Everest. He'd push himself up against the step, then stretch and strain to lift his shell onto the first level. Once there he'd pause for a moment to regain his strength, then repeat the same process with step two. As soon as he made it to the top he would be off at lightning speed (for a tortoise), determined to find his way back to Dad's vegetable patch.

Occasionally Tommy would fail to climb the steps and overbalance onto his back. Tortoises can die quite quickly if they aren't turned over. We'd often see him from the window, his legs scrabbling uselessly in the air, and Mum would yell at me to get outside and rescue him. If we went out for the day, we never knew whether to leave him in the yard or give him the freedom of the garden. If we chose the yard, we might return to find him on his back. But if he was allowed to roam, we'd need to make sure we were home before Dad so we could find Tommy and bring him back to the yard before his crimes were discovered. Chum was puzzled by this moving rock that we had in the garden and would often nuzzle Tommy with his nose, pushing him over onto his back and leaving him like that for us to find.

Then one day Tommy escaped. He had been restless for a while, desperate to get through the fence to mate with a female tortoise next door, and we returned from shopping to find that he'd dug his way under the fence and was nowhere to be seen. We searched and searched but it looked like he'd gone for good. Next door's female tortoise was missing too, and we suspected they'd eloped together into the allotments that backed onto our houses. We put up a notice offering a reward to anyone who found him, but there was no response. A month later, however, he turned up again in our garden, jaws stained very green from all the plants he'd eaten on his journey. He lived for a long time with my parents after I'd left home and had a family of my own. My older daughter, Karen, loved to feed him when she stayed at her grandma's house, and it was always one of the highlights of her visits.

The other pet that I remember from my childhood was a budgie called Joey. He was blue and black, quite lively and very vocal.

He lived in a cage on the sideboard, and once a day Mum would let him out to have a fly round the room. He'd perch on the curtain rail at one end of the room and then stretch his wings, take off and fly to the curtain rail at the other end of the room. He used to land on the table too, and play with his wobbly toys that we put there. Ducking and diving across the table, it would look as if he was dancing. Years later Joey would be the inspiration for my poem 'The Budgie Likes to Boogie'.

Budgies are supposed to be able to talk, but although we tried hard to get Joey to say 'Who's a pretty boy', we never met with success. When my parents were out, I attempted to teach him to say, 'Shut up', but he never managed it. Chum was irritated by Joey's flying across the room. On one occasion he put his nose up to the table and Joey pecked it. Chum kept his distance after that!

— CHAPTER FIVE —

Aunt Rose, Uncle Horace & Aunt Alice

Aunt Rose lived in a cottage in the Kent countryside. Just her house, the house next door, a farm down the lane, and then nothing till the village a mile and a half away. She was a small, stoutish, elderly lady, and we often spent our summer holiday with her. But there was one big disadvantage. Aunt Rose talked non-stop, mostly about things like knitting and jam making, things I wasn't the least bit interested in.

Aunt Rose could have talked for England. She was an Olympic winner in non-stop chat and everyone knew about her. The postman would draw up in his van, and I would see him looking into Aunt Rose's garden to see if she was about.

Then, when he thought she was nowhere around, he'd leave the safety of his van and scoot up the garden path. He'd push the letters through the letter box and be halfway to his van before she appeared. Then she'd call to him, ask him to do something for her, some little thing, anything, to keep him from getting back to his van, and that would be it for the postman.

Every time we stayed with Aunt Rose there'd be a morning when we'd wake up to find that cows had invaded her garden. The cows came from the field next door and would shoulder their way through a weakness in the hedge to munch away on her cabbages and lettuces. I'd be upstairs, looking out of my bedroom window, when the door downstairs would open and little Aunt Rose in her dressing gown would hurtle out like a rather dumpy superhero, down the garden towards the cows. Flapping a tea towel till it cracked like a whip, she'd bring it down on the backs of the cows, but they didn't seem to feel a thing. They were far too interested in her home-grown vegetables. Defeated, she would come back to the house, alternately muttering and yelling while she got dressed, before setting off down the lane to give the farmer a piece of her mind. This would happen every time. She had no phone, so she couldn't ring him, but it did seem strange to me that the slapping with the tea towel always had to be attempted before she'd go and fetch the farmer.

By far the very worst thing about staying with Aunt Rose was her outdoor toilet. It was really just a wooden box in a shed. Inside the box was a bucket. A round hole had been cut into the top of the box, and there you had to sit until what was needed to be done had been done. For someone used to an indoor bathroom with a flushing toilet, this was all too primitive. Occasionally it crossed my mind that someone had to empty the contents of the bucket when it got too full, but I quickly moved away from that thought. All I knew was that it sure wasn't going to be me!

(Recently in Norwich castle I discovered toilets, or 'garde robes', from Medieval times. These were very similar to Aunt Roses' toilet. Here, though, you sat in a row with friends and all did what needed to be done together, probably holding conversations about the weather or the high price of vegetables!)

Equally worrying were the spiders. As I sat in the shed I would be aware that all around me, hanging from corners and crevices, were spider webs. And where there were webs, there had to be spiders! I wasn't terrified of spiders, but I wasn't too fond of the larger ones. In the semi-darkness I'd convince myself that there were eyes watching me, small pinpricks of red in the gloom.

Worse still were the ones behind me, the ones I couldn't see and who were probably ganging up and planning a mass bungee jump the next time I entered their territory.

At night, of course, the house was locked up, so there was no way to get to the toilet outside even if I was brave enough to risk it. There was, however, a pot beneath the bed – a 'po', as Aunt Rose called it, or a 'gazunder' (because it goes under the bed!). If I woke in the night needing a pee, that was where it had to be done. And there it had to sit, beneath the bed, for the rest of the night. I hated it. In the morning I was supposed to carry the pot and its contents down Aunt Rose's narrow, twisty staircase and out to the toilet in the shed. No way was I going to do that! I knew what would happen if I tried to get down her stairs one-handed. I would be sure to slip and the contents of the pot would cascade all over me. There had to be a better solution.

So every morning when I woke, I opened my bedroom window, grabbed the pot and emptied its contents onto the flower bed beneath. I wasn't doing anything wrong – just following on from all those people in history who used to do the same thing. And they had emptied theirs out into the street, often over some unfortunate passer-by. All I was doing was watering the flowers. 'Strange,' Aunt Rose remarked one particularly dry summer, 'Those delphiniums under your window are looking very healthy.' I'm sure she knew what I was doing, but for once she kept quiet!

Whenever we stayed with Aunt Rose, we would take the train to Faversham, then catch a bus that would take us the seven miles to her house at the edge of a village called Wychling. Chum would be with us too, and he'd sleep in a special basket that Aunt Rose let us use, called a Moses basket. It always amused me that a basket could be named after our family name. Mum would remind me that the name came from the Bible. It was the sort of basket that the baby Moses would have been put into when they set him afloat down the river Nile. Looking at Chum sleeping peacefully in the basket, I'd think what a daft thing that had been to do!

Aunt Rose's house had no electricity. Every night, as it grew dark, she would fetch paraffin lamps and set them alight. Again, for someone used to light at the flick of a switch, this was a strange – and pongy – activity. The oil had a strong smell when it was first lit, and it took a while for our noses to get used to it. There was no television either, so evenings were spent reading, listening to the radio or playing cards. Then, when it was time for bed, candles were lit and carried upstairs. Candle light, of course, throws all kinds of disturbing shadows on the walls. I was a nervous child and often demanded that my mum sit with me till I'd fallen asleep.

Although there was much that worried me about staying with Aunt Rose, there were all sorts of games to play, places to explore and wild adventures to take part in. The woods were wonderful for camps. Each summer, the moment I arrived, I'd find a suitable site and spend the next week making my camp. I'd comb the woods for branches to make the framework, then cover it with bracken. Often there would be boxes that people had dumped in the woods, or even old car seats, and one summer I discovered a settee and chairs. Everything useful was dragged inside.

Another fun activity was to run with the rabbits in the field at the back of Aunt Rose's house. We would walk Chum across the fields each evening after supper, and he would race like a mad thing towards the scent of Rabbit City.

Before we arrived the rabbits would be peacefully munching grass in the evening sunshine. Then Chum would appear in their midst, abandoning any thought of stealth, succumbing to joyous barking as he chased them in every direction. He never caught any – they were far too quick for him – but he enjoyed the game. We'd walk on across the fields, then turn back so by the time we returned, the rabbits would have re-emerged and Chum could chase them a second time. That was the mark of a successful evening for our dog, who would then sleep contentedly in his basket for the rest of the night, whiffling and barking softly as in his doggy dreams he chased the rabbits all over again.

We only ever visited Aunt Rose in summer, but sometimes I'd look out of my bedroom window and imagine the fields stuffed with snow, the road blocked by drifts, and a weak winter sun barely clearing the trees. Somehow Aunt Rose got through the worst of the winter, camped out in her kitchen, knitted in mittens, with only the fug of the fire to ward off winter's chill. Once spring arrived she would pack up and visit us. 'I'm shaking the snow off my boots,' she'd say. And because she hadn't seen us all for so many months, she'd be telling us again how she shooed the cows that invaded her garden with a shout and a yell and the flap of a towel.

My nan (my mum's mother) lived for many years with her brother Horace in a house in Meeting Street. I called Horace 'Uncle', although he wasn't a real uncle. Whenever my mum and I went shopping we would call in on Nan and Horace to see how they were. They spent a lot of time playing with me, all sorts of games that must have been very repetitive and thoroughly boring for both of them.

Meeting Street was short in length, but it had Pickfords, a removal firm with big lorries that I enjoyed watching, and a church with a graveyard next door. There was a high wall around the graveyard, but from Nan's bedroom window I could see that beyond the wall there were graves in the grass that no one had tended for a long time. In the wall there was a tall black gate that was padlocked to keep the curious out (or to prevent anything sinister from escaping!). I dreamt up all sorts of fantasies about the place, at times frightening myself so much that I couldn't get to sleep at night. Years later, I don't remember when exactly, workmen came and cleared the graveyard, stacked the gravestones, then took them away. Houses were built on the site, but I was certain that no good would come from building houses in a graveyard. I imagined cracks forming in the ground, splitting the floors of houses while those inside were watching television. There'd be shrieks and screams as the carpet buckled, then burst apart as an arm reached up from the pit...

I was ten years old when my nan died. There were no mobile phones, or even a telephone in our house then, so my mum didn't find out straightaway. Horace had woken, taken his sister a cup of tea and discovered her dead. He'd told a next door neighbour, who cycled round to our house to deliver the news. My mum was distraught but tried to hold it in for my sake. Dad and Mum decided it was best if I went to school as usual, but I couldn't concentrate. I didn't go to the funeral either, but I do remember looking up at the clock and noticing it was eleven o'clock, the time that everyone would be saying goodbye to her. I rubbed my eyes to wipe away tears and then got on with my maths.

My mum and dad decided that Horace wouldn't be able to look after himself on his own, and it was agreed that he should move into our spare room. He kept himself to himself for much of the time, coming downstairs for meals and then going back up to his room. But every Sunday morning at ten o'clock precisely, he'd round up every pair of shoes in the house. He'd search beneath chairs, look inside cupboards, root through the dog's blankets till he felt sure that he'd found them all, and then he'd set them in a long line. There were, in those days, a lot of shoes that needed polishing, and Uncle would start at one end of the line and work vigorously till he reached the other end. It would take him a couple of hours, at which point he'd come and look for me. Then, like a general inspecting his troops, I'd walk down the line, examining the shoes and picking out any pair that wasn't as shiny as the others. Horace would give that pair an extra shine, put the shoes away, and go back to his room. But if I was too busy playing, or outside with my mates, or running about with the dog and just didn't feel like playing his game, he would get quite upset. 'Just play along with him,' Mum would advise me. 'Keep him happy.'

So I did, until he died a few months later. At this point, sensing a chance to make some much-needed money, I took over his job each Sunday morning. But I wasn't much good at it, and Dad was always complaining about how badly his shoes were polished. The memory stays with me, that smell of boot polish mixed in with the smell of the Sunday roast cooking in the kitchen. They were the Sunday smells of my childhood.

Aunt Alice was really my mum's aunt, but I called her Aunt too. She was a thin stick of a woman who always wore a black raincoat. Even on the hottest days of summer, she would be seen in town with her mac buttoned up to her throat. Whenever I talked to her, sooner or later she'd start moaning about the weather. If I remarked on what a lovely day it was, she'd sniff (Aunt Alice was a champion sniffer) and tell me that it was certain to rain the next day. She had the idea that life always balanced. Good weather one day meant bad weather another day. Good luck now would certainly result in bad luck coming along at some time in the future. But I liked Aunt Alice. I liked meeting her in the town because I could help carry her shopping home for her, and when we reached her house, I could spend some time with her parrot! Aunt Alice had the most amazing parrot, made doubly amazing by the fact that before he died, Aunt Alice's husband had taught that parrot to swear!

From the moment Aunt Alice turned her key in the door, the parrot would start squawking. I've never heard anything quite like it, before or since. It was definitely hands over the ears time! 'Oh you daft creature,' Aunt Alice would say as she moved towards the racket. She would drape a table cloth over the parrot's cage, and we'd wait for the squawking to subside. I'd move closer to the cage and, with my ear pressed to the cover, listen to the bird muttering to itself. Every now and then I'd hear a swear word. It was fascinating for me. When I was a boy people didn't swear as much as they do now; I learnt a lot from that parrot.

It was a wicked creature with eyes that followed me around the room and a curved beak like a scimitar sword. If ever I put my fingers too close to the cage, it would jab its beak into my flesh, drawing blood. I would howl and threaten the bird with all kinds of revenge, but its steely eyes would stare me out. It knew I was only bluffing.

But Aunt Alice could do whatever she liked with the creature. She could stretch her arm into the cage and the parrot would climb onto her wrist. She'd take her arm out and the parrot would edge its way along her arm and onto her shoulder. Then, like a pirate, like Long John Silver from *Treasure Island*, she would move round the room with the bird on her shoulder, gently nibbling her earlobe. But if I tried to get too close, if I moved my hand towards the parrot, it would jab me. And it was obvious from the wicked look in its eye that it had really enjoyed the attack!

CHAPTER SIX

Touch Your Toes

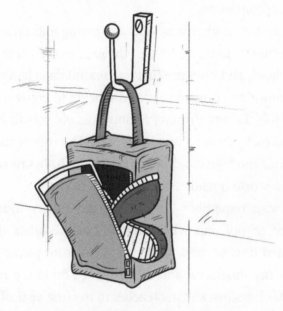

'**D**o I really have to go to school? Can't I stay at home with you?'

As the dreaded time when I would have to start school drew closer, my mum had to deal with such questions more and more. I can't remember whether there were playgroups or nursery schools when I was tiny, but either way, I certainly hadn't been to them. My mum had taught me my numbers and my letters, and I could already read simple words, so why couldn't I carry on learning at home? I didn't need school, particularly when my mum wouldn't be there with me. I was worried.

'Everybody has to go to school,' my mum told me. 'You'll make new friends. You'll enjoy yourself.' I still wasn't convinced.

But my teacher was kind and caring and understood the traumas that children go through in their first weeks of school, and after the first few tearful days had passed, my mum was proved right: I did begin to enjoy myself.

Holy Trinity Primary School was old – built in 1859 – and badly in need of a makeover. The rooms had high ceilings and high windows through which we saw nothing of the world outside except patches of sky.

I can remember little of the day-to-day routine of infant school, but when I came out the other side I'd learned how to read, to do sums, to paint pictures, and to tie my shoelaces, and then I moved on to the Juniors.

Mr Barstow was my teacher in my first year of junior school. He was very keen to tell us straightaway, 'You're in the juniors' now. Don't think you'll be getting any of that namby-pamby nonsense you got from the infants' teachers. It's time to grow up.'

What on earth was happening? We'd returned to school after the summer holidays to find that we'd entered a dragon's lair. Where was our safe and comfy classroom from last year? Where was the kind and lovely Mrs

Leach, who had cuddled us if we felt unwell and smiled the sort of smile that made us actually want to be at school? What on earth had we done to deserve Mr Barstow?

Mr Barstow was tall, with a bristling moustache and sharp eyes. Nothing got past him. If you were a boy and you'd done something wrong, then Mr Barstow would punish you. It didn't need to be anything serious: simply swinging on your chair or speaking out of turn or pinching someone in the playground was enough to get him going.

It was one Friday morning and we were in the middle of our end-of-the-week arithmetic test. I'd felt Caroline nudge me once already, but I tried to ignore it. She did it again and I knew she wouldn't leave it alone till I replied in some way.

'What do you want,' I hissed. It must have been louder than I'd meant to, as Mr Barstow strode across the room and glared down at me.

His voice thundered, 'Were you cheating boy?'

'No, sir, I wasn't, honest.'

If I said the word 'honest' to my mum, she knew I was telling the truth. Mr Barstow didn't work to the same rules. He'd already made up his mind.

'Stand up,' he bellowed.

I stood.

'Come with me.'

It was an invitation I didn't dare refuse.

I glanced at Caroline, briefly hoping she might say something, but she looked away. Everyone else watched me follow Mr Barstow to the cloakroom at the back of the classroom. He pointed in the direction of our PE bags.

I collected my bag and handed it to him. He took out one of my PE slippers.

'Touch your toes.'

I just couldn't believe that this was happening. It was unjust. It wasn't fair. I just wasn't guilty. Why wasn't somebody stopping this from happening? Where was my mum when I needed her? She wouldn't let him do this to me.

But there wasn't to be any last minute rescue. I bent down and touched my toes, or rather he put his hand on the back of my neck and forced me to bend down.

I wasn't prepared for the shock, the shock of being belted on the backside. Worst of all was the realisation that an adult could coldly and calculatingly inflict such pain and that we, as small boys, could do nothing to stop it. The first hit was an incredible surprise; it knocked me forward so that I toppled over. Before I had time to get over it, I was yanked up again and given a second blow. The third one was almost unbearable. That's when the tears came.

However hard I tried not to cry, it was no good. The tears were welling up inside me, and even though I squeezed my eyes as tight as I could, they still dribbled down my cheek. I don't know whether it was because of the pain from the slipper or whether it was just the humiliation of being singled out for such treatment. But at least I didn't sob. Boys who sobbed earned no respect whatsoever.

In all the comics I read, *The Bash Street Kids* and *Dennis the Menace* always managed to slip an exercise book into their trousers to absorb the blows they were given. Not so for us. That didn't happen in real life. We knew that much.

After the beating was over, it was incredibly difficult to go back to my place and sit down as if nothing had happened. Indeed, the last thing I wanted to do at that point was to sit down at all. Boys at my school quickly mastered the technique of hovering, of leaving a space between backside and seat. As I did so myself, it felt as if every pair of eyes were watching me, judging me, assessing how tough I was, how many tears there were. It was almost as if the rest of the class were holding up score cards, like they do for dance competitions. I waited to find out how I'd been rated.

There was one consolation however, and that was the knowledge that I'd now joined an elite bunch of boys who had been whacked. We wore a special badge of honour, or badge of dishonour perhaps. Other boys looked up to us, kept asking whether it hurt. Nobody, of course, wanted to admit that it had, so we stayed silent. Strong and silent, that was the impression we wanted to give. One or two boys were automatically leaders of this group, as they had forgotten their PE bags on the day they had the misfortune to be slippered, Mr Barstow had taken great delight in fetching his own slipper, which was, of course, twice the size and hurt twice as much (or so I was told. I always managed to remember mine, just in case!).

And, of course, Caroline was impressed, particularly so because I hadn't ratted on her. At lunchtime she gave me half of her wine gums as a reward.

When I went home that night, I didn't let on to my parents that I had been slippered. My dad was of the generation that believed teachers to be right whatever they did. He'd been whacked when he was a boy – often with a stick across chapped hands on winter mornings when he'd been late for school. He claimed that it had done him no harm. 'It made a man of me,' he'd say.

I knew boys who confessed to their mothers and were told in return, 'Just you wait till your father gets home.' They then spent several hours in anticipation of another thrashing. It was best to stay quiet and hope your parents wouldn't notice how you chose only the softest seats to sit on! I was lucky – I was an only child. For anyone with a brother or sister at school, the chances of keeping what happened a secret were minimal. Brothers might be bribed to keep quiet, but sisters were a law unto themselves. Many boys returned to school the next morning having spent much of the night dreaming up the most horrible revenge on sneaking sisters!

Beatings like this, painful as they were, paled to nothing when compared with the one that was given to David Aston in our final year of Primary School.

David wasn't a good mate of mine, although I hung out with him occasionally. At the time, though, I had been seeing more of him than usual, as he had been selling me some carriages for my train set. I had a huge train set that took up half of our loft. Dad had boarded the loft and helped me lay down track so that my trains could run in a complicated loop taking them through tunnels, past stations and up gradients. We built a whole town around the track, with shops, houses, a garage, a police station, fire station, a park and hills. It was a magnificent display that was the envy of all my friends.

One day David had turned up at school with a Pullman carriage, telling me that it was an unwanted present. Pullman meant luxury. These brown and cream carriages with their grey roofs were expensive models. They had names like Arcadia or Iolanthe, and I knew that even one Pullman carriage would add real class to my layout. I paid a couple of week's pocket money for it, and David told me that he might be able to get another one if I was interested. Other boys bought engines and carriages from David, and he seemed to have an unlimited supply of them.

Such was our desire for these toys that no one really questioned David as to why he had so many unwanted presents. But we were in for a huge shock at the next Monday morning assembly. We had just finished singing a hymn about loving God and loving one another, and had listened to our headmistress, Mrs Tyndall, as she praised the football team for their excellent results. Mrs Tyndall was ancient, always dressed in dark colours and rarely smiled. The chill in her voice as she spoke her next words soon spread over all of us.

'We now come to something very serious,' she announced, 'something very serious indeed.'

We looked at each other. We saw the teachers looking at each other. What was she on about? Just at that moment the door to the hall was flung open to reveal David being dragged kicking and screaming into the hall by Mr Barstow. Mrs Tyndall's voice cut through the racket, 'If you can't be quiet, David, it will be much worse for you.'

The effect on all of us was electric. We waited on the edges of our seats to see what was about to happen. 'This boy,' Mrs Tyndall almost screamed out, 'has been stealing. And not only has he been stealing, he has also been selling his stolen goods in my school playground.'

My heart seemed to stop beating as I heard these words, but I hadn't much time to think because Mr

Barstow was wrestling David to the floor, attempting to get him into a position where he could whack him.

Mr Mankelow, the year six teacher, moved to help him. Together they lifted David up, bent him double, and while Mr Mankelow headlocked him, Mr Barstow picked up the slipper (his own slipper on this occasion) and started to beat him.

Nobody spoke as Mr Mankelow released David, letting him fall to the floor. He was sobbing uncontrollably. 'I hope that will be a lesson to you, David,' said Mrs Tyndall. But at that moment David picked himself up and ran screaming at his headmistress. He beat his fists against her, and the words he hurled at her I had only heard spoken once before, and then from Aunt Alice's parrot.

We thought that Mrs Tyndall was about to have a fit. Her face turned purple with rage. She had obviously never been spoken to like that in the whole of her teaching life, and, certainly never in front of the entire school. If she were a saucepan, she'd have been boiling over. If she were a volcano, she'd have been blowing her top. She was fury on two feet. She was Trunchbull from Roald Dahl's *Matilda* long before he invented her. If we had been capable of worrying about anything else other than the sheer terror of the situation, we would have been concerned that she was going to have a heart attack. She was apoplectic. (Note to my younger readers: Learn this word and use it in your next English task. Your teacher will be really impressed!!!) She threw back her head and bellowed at Mr Barstow, 'GIVE THIS BOY SIX MORE.'

And David, realising that he had crossed some sort of uncrossable line, slipped to the floor and let his whole body go limp. Neither Mr Barstow nor Mr Mankelow could lift him into a position where he could be beaten properly, so Mr Burstow simply thrashed him where he lay, then left him there whimpering.

I felt physically sick. I think we all did, even those who had nothing to do with his crime. One or two of the girls were crying, but whether out of sympathy for David or simply because of the horrific spectacle we had just witnessed, I do not know. All I remember is that we filed out in silence, trying not to look at David still stuck to the floor. There was no noise in the classroom either. We just fetched our books and got down to our work. I do remember wondering what my teacher thought about what had happened. She was a gentle lady who gained her control of us through kindness. We felt guilty if we upset her in any way, and most of the time nobody wanted to anyway. She said nothing, but I just couldn't believe that she approved of what had taken place.

David didn't appear in class for the rest of the day. Rumour was that his mother had called and collected him, and that he wasn't to return to school for a week. Later our teacher spoke to us about David. She said that he'd be forgiven, that he would start again and put what had happened behind him. I just sat there and wondered if he would ever be able to forgive the ones who hurt and humiliated him.

When I got home that night, I dug a big hole in the garden. Rumour went round that if you dug deep enough and far enough, you'd eventually reach Australia. But I had no interest in testing that out; all I needed was a hole that was big enough and deep enough to bury a model Pullman carriage. 'Out of sight, out of mind,' as my mum would say. It's probably still there now.

— CHAPTER SEVEN —

Shut up & Watch The Match

In the boy's playground at school there was always a game of football going on, sometimes even two criss-crossing each other. One would be playing top to bottom and the other side to side. In the midst of these games would be a third group of boys acting out some battle scene involving Cowboys and Indians, or Brits and Germans. Although some boys would volunteer to be Indians, enjoying the chance to put feathers in their hair and run about uttering war whoops, it was much harder to persuade anyone to play the part of a German soldier. Quite often younger boys had to be 'persuaded' with the threat of Chinese burns or dead legs. ('Chinese burns' were when someone took hold of your arm with both hands and then twisted your skin sharply in opposite directions. Dead legs were the result of someone kneeing you in the fleshy part of your calf. It seemed to take all the strength from your leg for a few minutes.) It was best to try and avoid both of these playground tortures if you could.

There was no grass to play on and the playgrounds were tarmac, so grazed knees, cut hands, and knocked heads were inevitable. I was reminded of this recently when I visited a school and heard the first aider say to a queue of children, 'Don't bother me if it's scratched or patched, only if it's detached!'

Worse than anything the playground could inflict, though, was a knee to a certain tender place which could leave a boy rolling around on the ground in agony. It was the worst sort of pain followed by the worst sort of ache, and yet, despite having experienced it ourselves, we'd still laugh when it happened to someone else. There was little sympathy. I don't remember any swearing though, no matter what the injury, probably because we knew if we did swear and were overheard, there'd be an appointment with Mr Barstow's slipper.

Once, on the playground, a long line of us started joining hands forming a living lasso. This snaked its way round, encircling unfortunate victims, then contracting to crush them between us. As the lasso twisted and turned, those at the end would be flung around at great speed. So many boys needed medical treatment after being thrown into a wall by this that it was very quickly banned by our teachers.

The boy's toilet in the playground was a place where boys might demonstrate their skills in another area. Instead of using the urinals we would aim a stream of wee at the back wall to see how high we could mark it. This would leave very satisfying watery curves high up on the wall, and it was quite a contest to see who could make the highest mark. One boy claimed to have hit the roof, but it was generally thought that he must have cheated, as he couldn't repeat the feat with others watching. Later we discovered that he'd hidden a water pistol in his pocket.

For our football lessons we walked a mile, or what seemed like a mile, to a sports field where we could play. We all thought we were brilliant, but I only got into the first team on one occasion. I played regularly in team two, but in the few games that were arranged with other schools, we spent so much of our time fighting and bickering and bashing the keeper if he let a goal in, that before we knew it the opposing team would be up and at us again. We were embarrassing, our teacher told us, and he quickly gave up trying to teach us tactics. We had no idea about different positions – when the whistle blew, we all just swarmed after the ball.

But I do remember one game where our opponents were even worse than us. There was twice as much fuss each time their goalie let one through, and every time it happened they changed keepers. Soon we were winning eleven-nil and every one of their team had been in goal. We were mighty that night, we were world champions! If we'd have been planes we'd have looped the loop! We were going places, it was obvious. Our success, however, was short lived. Two weeks later we lost by a similar amount, and our dreams were just dreams once more.

When we played football, we all wanted to be our heroes in the teams that we supported. I started supporting Tottenham when I was ten. They were a great team in the early 1960s, winning both the league and the FA Cup in 1961, and the FA Cup again in 1962, Their opponents in '62 were Burnley. My mate Paul was a Burnley supporter, and we knew there'd be trouble when the Cup Final came round. In fact, it proved to be a real test of our friendship. I wrote about it in a poem:

Cup Final Day, 1962.

Paul supported Burnley,
but Spurs were all that I cared about.
We knew, by the end of Cup Final day
that one of us would be leaping about
and one of us would be quiet,
unless, of course, it went to a replay.

So that Saturday in May
we sat down to watch
the match of the year.

And Spurs got off to a dream start
when Jimmy Greaves scored an early goal
and I was ecstatic
till Paul knocked me back, 'Sit down,'
he said, 'Shut up, watch the match.'

It was nothing much till the second half,
then Burnley scored and Paul went mad,
but just as he sat back down again
it was Bobby Smith with a cracker of a goal
for Spurs. 'Don't shout so much,'
my mother called, 'the teams can't hear you.'

Then just ten minutes before the end
Blanchflower booted a penalty
and Spurs stayed in front 3-1.

I leapt around, jumped up and down,
ran round the room holding the cup,
listened to the sound of the Wembley crowd
as I took my victory lap.

'You're daft, you are, you're crazy,' Paul said,
but I jeered him all the way to the door,
'3-1,' I crowed, 'I told you so.'

Then, 'What shall we do tomorrow?' I called,
but he didn't turn round, just walked away,
and next day too it was like a wall
had suddenly grown between us.

He kept it up for a week or so,
wouldn't speak, kept clear of me,
and it took me a week to understand
that a game of ball didn't matter at all
it's friendship that really counts.
So I went across and knocked on Paul's door,
'I'm sorry that your team lost,' I said.
He shrugged. 'Doesn't matter anymore,
there's always next year, we'll beat you
for sure.'

'I expect so,' I said,
fingers crossed
behind my back.

A lot of boys at my school supported Ramsgate, but the local team held no interest for me. I was with the North Londoners. I listened each Saturday as the football results were read out on the television and noted the scores. My dad listened too, but for another reason. He wanted to see whether he'd won anything on the Football Pools.

Before the National Lottery there was the Pools. Each week players had to predict the results of football games. Points were given for successful predictions and these could add up to earn substantial cash prizes. My dad wasn't very good at predicting games and often asked me to do it. We never managed a major prize, although we did win small amounts on a couple of occasions. That didn't stop us dreaming, and whenever there was something that we had no hope of affording, either Dad or Mum or I would say, 'One day we'll buy it, when we win the pools.'

— CHAPTER EIGHT —

There's A Cow In My Bed

In my second year at school I was often ill. I think that I was one of the reasons my parents bought me Chum – they thought that a dog would help keep my spirits up. I had just had six weeks away from school with whooping cough, something that could prove quite dangerous for a young child, when the doctor prescribed some sea air. So every afternoon while my friends were at school, mum, Chum and I would trek along the beach while I breathed

73

in as much sea air as I could. It was an autumn designed to strengthen my lungs and get me fit again. Some afternoons I was desperately tired and found it hard to put one foot in front of the other. And then once we'd walked the beach, there was a long walk back across town to our house.

Once the illness had passed I returned to school in November, only to be off again with measles a couple of weeks later. Then Christmas came and went, and I went back to school for a week or two before falling ill for with pneumonia. This again could have dangerous complications for a young child, and my mum used to sit with me endlessly at night, mopping the sweat from my brow and reading me stories. I remember incredibly vivid dreams where I'd wake to find myself standing up in bed kicking my feet and desperately trying to escape the snakes that were slithering all over my sheets.

On another occasion I was convinced that there was a cow in my bed, and I was screaming at my mum to get it out!

It was another six weeks before I was anywhere near fit enough to return to school, and then it was only mornings for a while. I missed a lot of my year in the middle infants', but my mum did so much with me at home, getting me reading and writing, that when I returned I wasn't too far behind the others.

Soon after I'd shaken off the last of my three illnesses

that year, our relatives from Canada came to stay. Uncle Bert and Aunt Lily had moved to Canada in the 1920s and had been very successful in a city on the west coast called Vancouver. They appeared at our house with gifts for me: models of a wigwam and a totem pole actually made by American Indians, and, joy of joys, a remote controlled car. I loved that car, and played with it endlessly, walking round the room with the steering box in my hand while skilfully turning the car this way and that, around the table legs and under the chairs. Unfortunately the car lasted only as long as Uncle Bert and Aunt Lily's visit. It worked fine for the month that they stayed with us but then after a couple of days stopped working altogether. I was devastated. Dad knew how upset I was and took the car into a couple of toy shops to see if they could find out what had gone wrong with it. Nobody seemed able to fix it. 'It's American,' they said. 'Can't get the parts.'

In desperation Dad even took the car to the toy department at Selfridges in London. 'If they can't fix it,' he said. 'No one can.'

But they couldn't fix it, and the car was consigned to the toy cupboard. I could still push it around with my hands, but it wasn't the same. That car had been special.

Around this time I had my first real encounter with the dentist. I'd had my teeth looked at before, of course. Once a term we would have a dental inspection at school, and class by class we would all be lined up to wait our turn to 'Open wide'. For some reason, lack of space probably, these dental visits took place in our headteacher's office, which for a day became a dental surgery, while the head moved in with the school secretary. No actual surgery ever took place there, but if something that needed attention was spotted, then parents would be given an appointment to take their children to the real dentist's surgery in the town. Up till then, for me, there had never been anything to worry about, but on this occasion the dentist prodded and probed for much longer than usual, then asked his dental nurse to write down something in her record book.

This didn't look good to me, but when I told my mum she said not to worry and to wait and see if a letter arrived to give me an appointment. After about a week a letter did arrive. I needed to have some teeth removed as it was too overcrowded in my mouth and, if nothing were done my second batch of teeth would come through the gums at awkward angles. I was horrified. It was two weeks to the appointment, and I was dreading it.

My mum tried to reassure me by telling me that I would be given gas and so be asleep the whole time. The whole notion of being given gas wasn't comforting in any way. Didn't gas kill you if you breathed in too much of it? Didn't they use it as a weapon in World War One?

What on earth was the dentist up to?

I barely slept at all the night before the appointment. The dentist's surgery was a mile or so from our house, on the other side of town, and I counted the hours to the time we had to depart. Then, when there were no more hours left, I kept on counting the minutes: half an hour still, twenty-five minutes, and so on. I was a wimp, I knew, but on the way to the surgery I didn't care. I kept hanging back till my mum was almost dragging me along. The main road took time to cross, and we stood there waiting for a break in the traffic. Perhaps we'll be stuck here all day, I thought to myself, tooing and froing, jumping back to avoid the cars and lorries, never getting any further. But finally we got across.

Next came a long road that was nowhere near long enough. In the town itself, I paused at the pet shop to see if their puppies had been sold. 'No time,' my mum said. 'We'll be late. Look when we come back.'

Up the hill now and round the bend. I could see the harbour below me. 'If only I could sail away,' I thought. 'Jump a ship, be free...' But it was too late. We'd arrived, and I counted the steps – two, three, four – till mum reached out and rang the bell.

Then it was the waiting room, prolonging the agony even more, till my name was called and we were taken in to meet the dentist. I'm sure I was trembling as I climbed into his chair. I'm sure that I was looking across at my mum with sorrowful eyes, imploring her to find an excuse to stop what was about to happen. In all my favourite films, a hero always arrived at the last minute – to rescue someone tied to the railway tracks, to pull them from an out of control vehicle – carrying them off a second or two before the train rattles past or the car explodes. But there was to be no hero for me. The dentist was telling my mum what was to happen. I heard the word 'extraction' and it didn't sound good.

I could smell rubber and watched a big balloon like a football bladder inflating and deflating in front of me. Then a black mask was pushed over my face, and I heard a hissing sound and smelt the gas. After that, nothing, till I woke up with my mouth full of blood. I was told to spit it into the sink and then bite on a hard chunk of cotton wool till the bleeding stopped. All this time I felt wobbly, like one of my mum's jellies. The room seemed to be spinning and I felt sick.

Mum was there supporting me, and we went and sat in the waiting room till the spinning stopped and I was able to get to my feet without feeling as if I was about to collapse. I ran my tongue round my mouth and could feel the places where I no longer had teeth. Five had been removed, my mum told me.

We made it into the open air, where Mum wrapped a scarf round my face to keep out the cold, and walked slowly to my nan's house, where I was to recover while my mum went shopping. Nan and Horace fussed over me, but I could hardly keep my eyes open and soon fell asleep. When I woke my mum had returned with presents for me, for being a 'brave boy'. I didn't really feel I'd been brave – I'd had no option. One thing I knew though: I would never, ever be going anywhere near that dentist again. In fact I was twenty-eight when I finally lost my fear of the dentist, and I then stayed with the same one for the next thirty years. He was kind, gentle, considerate and it was almost a pleasure to visit him.

If there was anything I was more scared of than the dentist, it was the big needle used for immunisations. Nothing could bring out the wimp in me quicker than when our teacher gave out letters at the end of the day and, scanning them quickly, I would see the dreaded word vaccination.

According to the doctors, it made real sense to vaccinate everyone. You would be given a little drop of a virus and be safe from catching the full blown sickness. There were killer diseases like diptheria and scarlet fever, and others like polio, which if it didn't kill you would leave you crippled in some way. And rumour was that you could catch polio from swimming pools, from crowded places like cinemas and from using public drinking fountains.

So when I complained about having a vaccination, my mum would remind me of a Victorian red brick building on the outskirts of our town called Haine Hospital, where children went if they caught scarlet fever or other infectious diseases. It was an isolation hospital where anyone with such a disease could be kept away from other children. Anyone who visited had to wear protective clothing and masks for fear of spreading it further. Anything that a patient brought into the hospital could not be taken away again. Everything had to be burnt. It sounded grimmer than grim, but although I knew I never wanted to go there, I was still equally as terrified of the injections that could help me avoid it.

The problem was, of course, that we heard so many horror stories about injections. Ben's brother couldn't move his arm for weeks, it was so painful. He had to wear it in a sling. It went something called 'sceptic' where they rammed the needle in. The needle was huge, like a bicycle pump. Three nurses were needed to hold him down. He'd been gagged and blindfolded and the needle jiggered and jumped around like a road drill!

My dad didn't help. He'd tell me stories of his army days where men were lined up in rows. 'Thump, thump, thump,' he'd say. 'When it got to you the needle was blunt!' Mum told him not to be so stupid. Couldn't he see how worried I was?

'Even lorry drivers faint sometimes,' someone had once told my mum when she had a blood test. So how was I supposed to be brave? All I knew that the clock was ticking away the days and hours till I'd have to face the needle myself. I just couldn't understand how when they punctured my skin, the blood didn't just gush out, and keep on gushing out till there was no more left!

On the day itself I pretended I had all sorts of problems – headache, stomach ache, sore throat – anything to get me off school. Mum threatened to take me in herself and stand there waiting with me. That wouldn't do, I knew that. All the boys would laugh at me, even though they were just as worried. I had to face up to it by myself.

'It's just a pinprick,' our teacher assured us. 'Hurts for a second and then that's it.'

What I do recall, after all these years, is that the nurses who gave us the injections were mostly very kind. They spoke reassuringly and tried to be as gentle as they could, knowing we were mostly terrible cowards who might well burst into tears at any minute.

There was the smell of what I was told was 'antisceptic', followed by a kind word and then the pinprick. I could feel the tears welling up and squeezed my eyes tight to stop them falling. I couldn't look, have never been able to look, even though injections hold no fear for me now. And then, it was over. Cotton wool was pressed to my arm and a plaster applied. 'Now, that wasn't anything to worry about,' the nurse smiled.

I felt a wonderful relief. All the worry and the awful

apprehension of the past two weeks slipped from my shoulders, and for the first time in days, I smiled.

At other times we'd stand in line for the nit nurse. She always looked stern and unfriendly. Maybe it was the nasty job she had to do that made her seem so unpleasant herself. Her fingers in your hair were anything but gentle, and if you moved an inch while she was checking you, she would roughly pull you back again. If she failed to find any nits, it seemed to us that she would be disappointed. On the occasions that she did, she would crush the creature between her thumb nails while grunting, 'Got you.' Those who were found to have nits were grouped together on one side of the hall. Their parents were summoned and all the family could then look forward to an unhappy appointment with a bottle of nit lotion and a steel comb. 'Make sure you see who has nits and then keep clear of them,' my mum would tell me. 'Don't bring them home here.' My evasion tactics must have been successful, as I don't believe I ever did.

One problem I did suffer from was a digestive system that didn't always seem to work as it should. My mum would ask me each morning, 'Have you been?' She wanted to know if I'd done a number two, as she called it, but I would often play dumb and reply, 'Been where?' Sometimes days went by and I would fail to answer yes to her question even once. Then my mum would start offering me all kinds of aids to get 'things moving again', as she put it. She would appear with a bag of liquorice from the corner shop and watch to make sure I ate some of it. Prunes were another option. Prunes are dried plums and were supposed to help a sluggish system. Then there was the dreaded last resort of milk of magnesia, a foul-tasting white liquid which would ensure that you spent the next day in the loo, bored out of your skull, while your system 'regulated' itself!

CHAPTER NINE

The Bogeyman Will Get You

I hated the dark when I was young. I hated that time at night when I had to stop reading, when Mum came and pulled the book from my hands and I begged for five more minutes. 'Aww, go on Mum,' I'd plead, 'Just let me finish my chapter, just let me read to the bottom of the page...' It was all delaying tactics, just to put off that moment when the light would go out. 'Can I have a glass of water? Can you rearrange the covers? I'm too hot. Can you get me a hot water bottle? I'm cold.' Anything to keep my mum from turning the light off.

To get to my room I had to pass by three chambers of blackness, three rooms with open doors where all kinds of demons might be lurking. Then, once inside, I'd check the wardrobe, peer beneath the bed and open the door of the walk-in cupboard, terrified in case something walked out. Then, having got into bed, I'd feel that terrible urge to get out and check again, just in case I'd failed to spot something lurking in the corners, something small just waiting for the light to go out before it began to grow in size. I'd imagine arms, tentacles, claws reaching out and up from under the bed, moving towards my throat, about to strangle me. The dressing gown that hung on the back of my door had to be removed before I could sleep. To me, in the darkness it resembled the folded wings of some huge bat-like creature that would uncurl itself the moment the light disappeared, then flap over to the bed and sink its fangs into my neck!

I would imagine I'd heard noises from the cupboard – rasping breath, rattles and rumbles. I'd picture the lock springing open to reveal something so monstrous that I couldn't begin to describe it. On windy nights, the loft hatch on the landing would shift and scrape, and again I'd picture some nightmare creature clawing its way out, dropping down to the floor and then heading towards my room.

I couldn't sleep without the landing light on and my door partly open to allow a blade of light to slice through the darkness. But that, of course, was an open invitation for the Bogeyman to come calling...

My mother didn't invent the Bogeyman. She only ever joked about him, and she really didn't use him to scare me. But I *was* scared. – '*If you don't hurry up and get to sleep, the Bogeyman will be after you...*' '*If you don't stop biting your nails the Bogeyman will get you...*'

It seems that the threat of the Bogeyman has been used by parents for many years, and is still used in many countries today. In the Mid-west of the USA, the Bogeyman scratches on the window pane at night. In other places he hides under the bed or in the cupboard and comes out to tickle you. In many countries he's a man with a sack on his back who carries off naughty children.

But where did the name come from and what on earth did he look like?

Like all boys, I'd done my fair amount of nose picking. It was something to do when you were bored, when there was nothing else to do. Stick a finger up your nose and wriggle it round and pull out a bogey or two. I suppose because I was well fed, I never ate what I found there, and I was always quite revolted by the boys who did.

So was the Bogeyman made of bogeys? Would I find

him sliming his way towards me, slithering across my bedclothes to cover me in slime until I was caught, wrapped up like a fly in a spider's web? And would I still be alive, desperately trying to punch a way out of the giant bogey he'd trapped me inside?

Many a night I'd wake from a nightmare to find myself screaming, standing up in bed holding the sheets and calling out for my mum.

She'd be there pretty quickly. The light would be on and she'd be holding me, calming me, telling me it was only a dream. But it always seemed all too real to me.

Mention the Bogeyman by day, to your mates, and they'd fall about laughing. But at night, on your own, in the less-than-comforting darkness, you couldn't be certain.

The Bogeyman lives
in his bogey room,
with his bogey wife
in the bogey gloom.

With his bogey kids
and his bogey dreams,
and his house at night
full of bogey screams.

Drains in the street were another source of fear. I imagined gruesome black shapeless creatures smelling of death and decay, crawling out from between the gaps in drain covers, finding their way into my house, up the stairs and into my bedroom. These nightmarish creatures were obvious relatives of the Bogeyman, and just waiting to invade my mind the moment I closed my eyes.

You can play outside but don't mess about
near drains – my mother's advice
as I unlatched the gate and looked for lessons
the street could teach me.

The nasty boys up the road looked
into drains, they reached down and fisted out
pennies. I knew they'd fall prey
to some terrible plague.

Later I learned to drop bangers down drains,
held them fused till they almost blew
then let them fall to the muck below,
hearing the CRUMP of some deep explosion.

Sometimes tankers came to the street
and workmen lowered hoses, thick as anacondas,
to slurp and sway till the drains were dry.

All my nightmares slunk from drains,
their bulbous heads and shrunken forms
danced shadows on my walls.

Mother said there was nothing, no need
for worry at all. She talked away devils
and held back the night, but still my doubts
came crowding back – not everything
my mother said was right.

I also had bad dreams about falling. I'd be up, somewhere high, a tall building or on top of a cliff, and far too near the edge. And the ground would give way and I'd be falling, tumbling, turning head over heels, down, down, down to the rocks below. But I never reached them. I always woke just in time.

Later on there were nightmares about railway tracks, about the underground trains in London. I'd be standing on the platform edge looking at the rails, and then suddenly I'd be down there, looking up at the platform. And the rails would start to tremble and I'd hear a rumble that grew to a roar as the train approached the station. I'd curl myself into a ball and hope there'd be room for me to survive below the train...

At night I was a scaredy-cat, I was yellow, I was chicken. I longed to draw strength from the heroes I read about or watched on TV, to have just a fraction of Robin Hood's bravery or be as bold as Sir Lancelot.

My mum knew a rhyme that she'd often recite before turning out my light:

From ghoulies and ghosties,
and long-legged beasties
and things that go bump in the night,
Good Lord deliver us.

Or sometimes she'd say another favourite:

Sleep tight,
don't let the bed bugs bite.

Bed bugs... how big were they, I wondered.

But nothing quite matched the day my dad took me to London to visit the British Museum. I was bored by a lot of it – Greek and Roman statues, pottery, tapestries, old books – and realising this, my dad decided that he'd show me the Egyptian galleries. The mummy cases were huge, with fabulous pictorial writing (hieroglyphics) all over them. But some of the cases were open revealing the twisted and tangled remains of people who had once been human, but were now mummified out of all recognition. I backed away and refused to look at any more, much to my dad's disappointment.

These creatures fuelled my nightmares for years after. When I closed my eyes, I could see their sunken eyes, shrunken limbs, their brown bandages and their twisted smiles, or so it seemed.

— CHAPTER TEN—

Pink Shrimps & Jamboree Bags

There was a corner shop at the end of my street. It was owned by Mr and Mrs Peete, who were known to my parents as Norman and Gwen.

Mr Peete was often unwell. This was the result of being held in a Japanese prisoner of war camp for much of World War Two. My mum used to say that when he came back, his wife hardly recognised him. A starvation diet had left him 'just skin and bone'. Mrs Peete too was unwell. She suffered with a condition known as multiple sclerosis, which is a wasting away of the muscles, and her husband would have to carry her from the car to her chair in the shop. But for all they suffered and had suffered, this couple were two of the gentlest, kindest people I've ever met. I was always welcome in their shop. They were interested in what I was doing and would often press a sweet or two into my hands as I left.

The sweet display in their shop was a real treasure trove for kids. In summer you would have to fight your way past the wasps, but it was worth risking a sting to grab a handful of sugary treats.

Liquorice was a great favourite, and I was also always drawn to the 'Popeye the Sailorman' pipes and the Catherine wheels, which could be unwound and dangled into your mouth.

Gobstoppers, or 'Jawbreakers' as they're known in the USA, were a good buy as they would last and last. You could start sucking a gobstopper mid-morning, take it out for lunch, suck it again all afternoon, break for tea and then keep sucking till you went to bed. What was left could then be placed carefully on the bedside table till the next morning. I say 'carefully' because you didn't want it to roll off in the night and find it covered in dust and dog hairs.

I was particularly keen on two small chews known as Fruit Salads and Black Jacks. Fruit salads were a mixture of raspberry and pineapple flavours, while Black Jacks were aniseed and left you with a tongue that was satisfyingly black! There were aniseed balls, too, that could be sucked over a long period of time or hidden away in pockets to be found at a later date. Children could also buy sweet cigarettes made of white sugar with one end coloured red. Pink shrimps were a great favourite too. They were incredibly sweet and probably a dentist's worst nightmare, but it was hard to resist them.

All the unwrapped sweets sold for a half-penny each, and I'd stand before them for ages, clutching my pennies, trying hard to decide which ones I wanted in my bag.

Another temptation were jamboree bags. These were bags that held four or five small sweets, a tube of sherbet or a liquorice stick, plus a cheap toy. You never knew what you were getting so it was a bit of a gamble. Often, what the bag held was a great disappointment – a badge, a ring, a small plastic car – but there was always the hope that next time you bought one the contents would be different.

Behind the counter, arranged on shelves, were big jars of sweets. You had to ask specially for these and buy enough to fill a small bag. The choice was huge: barley sugars, bulls eyes, winter mixture, humbugs, mints, toffees, wine gums, jelly babies, sherbet lemons, liquorice allsorts, rhubarb and custard, sugared almonds, jelly beans, chocolate limes, hazelnut whirls and so on.

When I think about the huge amount of sweets that I ate as a boy, I am surprised that I have any teeth left in my mouth!

Living in a seaside town, there was always plenty of seaside rock for sale, long sticks of the stuff with the town's name – Ramsgate – written through the middle of it. I loved the pink-covered peppermint flavour, but there was also pineapple, lime, and a multi-coloured stick that looked attractive but somehow didn't live up to its promise. And all courtesy of the single best place in all our seaside town: The rock shop.

This was a shop just off the seafront that only stocked rock and related sweet stuff: humbugs, lollies that would crack your teeth if you were foolish enough to bite into them, candyfloss, false teeth, sugar mice, sugar dummies. When you entered the shop the smell was just heavenly. Just like sniffing a dream!

And I did dream of the rock shop. We all did. We mainly dreamt of being locked in there at night. How we were going to achieve that I didn't know, but that wasn't the point. In our dreams we were there, the shop empty, and so many sweet treats to taste and enjoy. In my dream I'd be just getting started, licking the biggest sugar lolly that I could find, and then suddenly, hey presto, I'd wake up. Then no matter how hard I struggled to get back to sleep, to find my way back to the dream, I could never do it. I'd have similar dreams about being locked in toy shops, but the rock shop was my favourite.

Wonder of wonders, too, you could actually watch the sweets being made. There was a long table or counter that ran the length of the side window, and the shop assistants, always white cloaked and gloved like surgeons at some operation, would roll out lengths of soft candy and skilfully stretch and twist them into long tubes. As they did this, a crowd of kids with their tongues hanging out would gather at the window, desperate to taste what was being prepared in front of them. The assistants would take up knives, cut the candy to the lengths they needed, then place it on trays and take the trays to the huge ovens in which the candy would be baked hard. For us kids, it was a glimpse of heaven, especially if we were then allowed inside, not just to feast our eyes but to actually choose what we fancied.

There were other sweet treats too. Once a week the toffee apple man would appear in our street, calling out what sounded like 'Torfee apples.' For mums who failed to interest their children in eating fruit, these were the next best thing, although they can't have been very healthy when covered in so much sugary toffee. You'd need to be careful as the toffee was baked so hard that it could easily crack a tooth. Of course, if you were desperate to get rid of a tooth that was proving reluctant to drop out of your mouth, then biting on a toffee apple was often the solution. You just had to make sure that you didn't lose the tooth or the Tooth Fairy wouldn't pay you a call. Most of us, of course, didn't really believe that the sixpence under your pillow was left by a fairy, but you didn't want to express too much doubt just in case there was something in it and she passed you by! Sixpence bought a lot back then! For example, a huge amount of sweets to eat during Saturday morning pictures.

Every Saturday morning around nine thirty a noisy queue would begin to snake down from the cinema and back along the High Street.

Kids from all over town were waiting for the doors to open. As soon as they did there was a great surge forward as everyone piled into the foyer, the doorman desperately trying to keep order. But it was like trying to hold back a tidal wave. He'd be valiantly attempting to get one part of the crowd under control while kids who hadn't brought money would be waiting till his back was turned so that they could nip upstairs to the balcony. With no tickets to show, they'd be waiting till the usherette was guiding others to their seats, and then slip by unnoticed. I can't think that the number of bodies in the cinema ever matched the number of tickets sold.

Another way of getting in without paying was through the windows of the gents' toilet. Someone already inside the cinema would go into the toilet and open the window so that a number of skilful climbers could be bunked up from outside.

As we waited for the show to begin, the noise would be incredible. Kids would be chanting, cheering, yelling out to others, kicking the backs of seats and stamping on the floor, till at ten o'clock the lights would go down and the cinema manager in suit and tie would edge nervously onto the stage. This would be the signal for those sitting nearest the front to begin enthusiastically shooting peas at him from shooters that they'd hidden in their pockets. He'd quickly start doing a dance, like a puppet on jerky strings, trying to avoid the missiles. 'If this doesn't stop,' he'd call out, 'there will be no programme this morning.' This announcement was met with jeers and catcalls. Why he persisted in trying to welcome everyone each week I never knew. He must have lived in fear and dread of Saturday morning pictures. Bet he never slept much on Friday nights!

There were always cartoons to begin with – *Mickey Mouse, Donald Duck, Goofy* – followed by *Laurel and Hardy* or *The Three Stooges*. Then there would be a serial, a new episode each week, all of them with the sort of cliff-hanging, edge-of-the-seat, heart-stopping final moment that was guaranteed to bring you back next week. All week we'd be talking about it, how our hero had been left hurtling towards a waterfall with a monumental drop to a whirlpool below, or hanging by his fingernails from a ledge where one wrong move would send him plummeting to the wild and raging river. The main feature was often *Zorro*, with his flashing sword blade, *Robin Hood* (feared by the bad, loved by the good) or cowboys like *The Lone Ranger*, *Roy Rogers* or *Hopalong Cassidy*. Other weeks it was *Flash Gordon*, *Superman* or *Batman*, all intent on saving the world from certain destruction.

And then, of course, the film projector would break down, plunging us into darkness. The shouting and screaming would begin at once, while the manager slipped out from behind the curtains and beg for calm till the film started up again. Then, when it was all over, we'd fountain out into the streets, whooping and hollering our way back home, reliving in our games what we'd watched on the screen.

CHAPTER ELEVEN

Dead Bait's Dead Useless

When I was ten or so, I developed an interest in fishing. Ramsgate harbour had two piers and the lighthouse pier was the one we fished from. But before we could go fishing, we needed to find bait.

In the evenings my dad and I would go bait digging. Finding our own bait meant that I didn't have to ask him for money to buy some, and my dad was always very keen on saving money where he could. Tide tables needed to be examined to make sure that it was low tide, as the best bait was to be found in the wet sand between the high and low water marks, and the best place to dig it was at the end of Ramsgate's western promenade. Dad would tie a garden fork to the crossbar of his bike, and with a plastic bucket hanging from his handlebars and the bait tin in his saddlebag, we would cycle across town and onto the prom.

When we reached the end, we chained and padlocked our bikes to the railings, untied the fork and dropped it down to the sand below. Then we clambered down a rusty iron ladder with several rungs missing and a final drop to the sand where the ladder had disappeared completely. Dad always insisted he went down first so that if I missed my footing he'd have a chance of catching me as I fell. I always thought it more likely that me falling on him would knock him off the ladder too, but I kept this thought to myself. If we'd really wanted to play safe, we could have walked a short way to where steps led from the prom to the beach. But climbing down the ladder somehow made it more of an adventure.

Once on the Sands we walked out to where the sand was wet. We were on nodding terms with the other fishermen, but everyone kept a careful distance from everyone else. It made me think of grainy pictures I'd seen of men digging for gold in California. Everyone had staked their claim to a patch of land, and trespassing would not be tolerated.

It was hard work for Dad, digging into the wet sand, but he dug quickly, turning it over with his fork. We were looking for lugworm and had to dig deep to find them. They burrowed through tunnels in the sand, and when we glimpsed one we'd have to break up the sand around the worm and ease the creature free. I don't think my dad liked this part of the activity, as he rarely handled the worms, preferring to leave it to me. They were wet and fat and unpleasant to handle as I slipped them into the tin, but slowly we accumulated a wriggling mass to be used as bait the next day.

Then Dad would straighten up, lean on the fork and rest from his labours. We'd watch the sunset, the sun slipping behind the silhouetted towers of Richborough power station, and I would always be amazed at how our shadows were lengthened by the low sun till we seemed to have the shadows of giants.

Then when the sun had gone and the day was growing dark, we'd put the lid on the tin and head back to the ladder. Me first, once more, with the climb always more difficult as we had the fork, bucket and bait tin to bring up with us. But it was worth it.

I went fishing nearly every day in the summer holidays. I'd cycle to the pier, my rod tied to the crossbar and my saddlebag bursting with bait, reels, tackle and sandwiches. Most days my mate Mike came too.

The best time to fish was just before high tide and just afterwards. High tide would bring in fish to feed on the shrimps that lived by the side of the pier. Looking back on it now, I'm not sure how I ever managed to bait my hook, but I did. Basically you couldn't just hook a worm. If you did, it would come loose from the hook straightaway, and you'd be fishing with an empty hook. The technique was to thread the worm along the hook, and in this way it would stay on the hook for the maximum amount of time, hopefully until it was gobbled up by an unsuspecting fish. Older fishermen would reassure me, 'Lugworm are cold blooded, they don't feel anything.' I knew I should check this out, confirm whether it were true or not on some scientific database, but I didn't. It was cruel, I'm sure, but small boys – me included – were cruel to small creatures all the time.

With the hook baited we would cast our lines as far as we could over the side of the pier wall, listening for the splash of the weighted hook and bait hitting the water.

Our fishing rods were then rested against the pier wall, and a peg with a bell clipped to the top of each. If we got a bite, the fish would pull on the line as it tried to get free, and the bell would ring. Then there would then be the struggle to reel the fish in before it managed to escape.

We caught a lot of crabs too, really big ones, the kind that you see in fish shop windows. They were great fun. We would wait until people started walking along the pier and then release them. The crabs would scuttle sideways, claws uplifted like baseball catchers, and the shrieks from the passers-by when faced with these armoured creatures were wonderful to hear. We'd make sure to grab the crabs before they fell back into the water, and take them back for a second run.

You do, of course, have to know how to handle crabs, particularly the large ones. We'd practised for years with the smaller ones in rock pools, and it's basically the same technique. You need to spread your hand wide and clasp the crab with thumb and forefinger at each side of its body behind its two wicked claws. This prevents the creature from moving its pincers into a position where they can give you a nasty nip.

One day Mike cast off, only to see his tackle fall into the sea close by as an enormous tangle of line burst out of his reel. After half an hour I was all for cutting the line adrift and starting again with fresh tackle, but Mike didn't like to be beaten. He pulled and pushed, twisted the line and curled it round his hands until, after what seemed like ages, he stood up smiling and began to reel in his line.

But all of a sudden he looked puzzled and handed the rod to me. I pulled on the line and could feel something heavy. We looked over the pier to find that the line had drifted right into the wall. We pulled again and this time felt movement. Slowly, very slowly, we hauled in our catch. I could hardly believe it. 'It's a lobster, a huge one!'

It was huge too. It hadn't taken the hook in its mouth but had somehow become caught up in the line. Untangling this from around the creature's wicked pincers was dangerous work, but finally we had it free. It lay there blowing bubbles and staring at us. 'You want to sell that,' we heard a voice say, 'There's any number of pubs who'll buy it.'

I had a basket fixed to the handlebars of my bike, and we managed to wedge the lobster inside it with one pincer waving free. Then we set off along the pier and into the town.

The landlord of the Rose and Crown was busy in the bar when we arrived, holding our lobster wrapped up in a towel. 'Out!' he shouted. 'You're not allowed in here!' Round the back we ran into his wife, who took one look at us and shook her head.

We tried the King of Denmark. There was a sign in the window that said 'Crab salads'. This time we went straight round the back, where we found the landlord washing glasses. He showed us a tank of crabs and a couple of lobsters. 'More than enough to last me here,' he said. 'Try Charlie at the Red Lion.'

But by the time we found Charlie, Mike didn't seem keen to hand the lobster over. 'What'll happen to it?' he asked.

'Well,' Charlie replied, 'the only way to cook a lobster is to boil it alive. You put it in cold water and then gradually bring it to the boil. You need a big pan as it'll be moving around for a while. Lobsters take a long time to die.'

I looked at Mike and he looked at me. We both looked at the lobster. It was still blowing bubbles. 'I'll pay you five shillings,' Charlie offered, reaching out to take the lobster. Five shillings! That wouldn't even buy us a packet of bait for tomorrow's fishing. I shook my head. 'No thanks, mister.'

We cycled back to the harbour, picked up the lobster and inched our way down a slipway. Unwrapping it from the towel, we eased it into the water.

It floated around for a bit and didn't look too happy. We thought it was dead, but finally, with a flip of a claw, almost as if it were waving, it sank below the water. We watched as bubbles rose to the surface. Later I wondered what the creature might have said to its family, how it might have explained what had happened. 'You'll never guess what sort of day I've had...'

Years later, when I watched the film *E. T.*, I recognised us, that moment when we cycled through town with an alien creature in the bicycle basket. We didn't actually take off into the air, but we did whiz down the hill so fast that at times we thought we might!

Another fishy tale is a story told to me by my nan. Every family has its own folklore, stories that get handed down from one generation to the next, and the one my nan told me concerned her brother Bert when he was young. It seems that Bert was even keener on fishing than I was. He'd be down at the harbour everyday and needed a constant supply of fresh bait to keep him going. You could buy dead bait, of course, but if that was ever suggested, Bert's reply was always the same, 'Dead bait's dead useless. You can't fool fish.'

When he couldn't get any lugworm, Bert would spend a lot of time searching the rock pools, filling a bucket with small crabs. Ready for a long day's fishing, overnight he'd keep the crabs in a bucket filled with sea water and sand in the yard. One night, it seemed that the crabs somehow managed to escape from the bucket. I could imagine them giving each other a bunk up, climbing on each other's backs till somehow they'd clawed their way out. Then with a sideways hop and a long legged dance across the yard, they disappeared through a gap beneath the door of the outside toilet.

This was just the moment when Bert's grandma had chosen to have some quiet time on the loo prior to going to bed (there was no indoor toilet in those days). So Grandma, caught with everything down round her ankles, watched horrified as a line of follow m'leader crabs edged towards her and vanished between the folds of her skirt and petticoat.

Apparently the scream that she let loose was heard

down at the harbour. It was certainly heard by everyone in the street – that is, apart from Bert's grandad, who had fallen asleep. He knew nothing of what was happening until there was a pounding on the front door, and several neighbours in nightclothes all asking if there'd been a murder.

Everyone raced through the house to the back yard, where the toilet door was flung open to reveal Bert's grandma standing on the toilet seat and whimpering to herself. She had raised her skirt and was shaking it vigorously to remove the crabs which clung there.

Bert was summoned from his bed, cuffed round the head and told to round up the creatures. 'If anything like that happens again,' Bert's grandad warned him, 'I'll slipper the seat of your pants so you won't sit down for a week.'

Bert grinned to himself, but thought it best to remove the paper package of freshly dug lug from his grandma's cool cupboard, just in case. (There were no fridges then, so a cool cupboard was a cupboard in a shady spot, where milk and cheese were kept to try and stop them going off.)

CHAPTER TWELVE

Count Reindeer

'Christmas, bah! Humbug!' That was the view of the miser Scrooge in *A Christmas Carol* by Charles Dickens. It put me off ever reading the book as a child. Why would anyone hate Christmas? Christmas was a wonderful time, a magical time. An occasion when your dreams might come true. Each year around September I would begin preparing my wish list. Although my mum often told me that Christmas isn't just about presents, I found it hard to think otherwise. I would be adding to and subtracting from the list right up to December 1st, which was when I'd need to give Mum my final version. Even then I'd often try to squeeze something in at the last minute.

What was puzzling about Christmas, however, was the whole Father Christmas thing. There was a Santa in the big store in Ramsgate and another in the store in Margate. There were Santas on the TV. But which, if any, was the real Santa? Mum said that they were all helping the real Santa because it was impossible for him to be everywhere at once. But he managed on Christmas Eve, I thought to myself. There must be some magic involved.

Without magic, how could one man visit every house in the world in one single night? There were, my dad said, over three thousand houses in Ramsgate alone. So how many houses must there be in the whole country? In the whole world? Nobody could do it. It was impossible. Surely somebody must be telling huge porky pies. And what about all those mince pies and glasses of sherry that everyone left out for Santa? Even with the help of Rudolph and the rest of the reindeer, they'd never get through that lot. It was mystifying. And all this business about coming down chimneys? My friend Richard didn't even have a chimney and he still got presents! And my parents always left the coal fire smouldering overnight so they wouldn't have to spend time relighting it on

Christmas Day. Surely Santa would scorch his bum if he tried anything with our chimney!

One year I discovered a pile of wrapped presents with my name on at the back of Dad's wardrobe. I was caught, of course, so engaged was I with the shaking of these presents to see if they rattled. Mum, thinking I'd been quiet for some time, too quiet to her mind, had sneaked quietly up the stairs and found me. Even she didn't believe me when I suggested that I'd just been seeking a route through to Narnia and had stumbled upon the presents by accident.

There was an obvious reason why the presents were there, she told me. Parents bought the presents, wrapped them and then passed them on to Father Christmas so he could deliver them on Christmas Eve.

'Don't tell your dad.' Mum warned me. There were lots of times when Mum and I kept a secret from Dad, although at other times, when I did something wrong, she'd say, 'I don't know what your dad will say.' And when she got really annoyed with me, she'd threaten, 'Just you wait till your dad gets home.' Other kids might have quivered at this, but my dad never really got angry. He'd huff and puff for a bit, and I might get sent to my room for half an hour, but nothing more. (I only remember one occasion when he walloped me, and I think it upset him more than it did me. Whatever it was for, I've long forgotten, but I'm sure I deserved it!)

Each year before Christmas there would be a toy procession through the streets of Ramsgate, presided over by Father Christmas himself.

This was a charity event where children were supposed to wrap up a toy they didn't play with anymore, then hand it in at the toy procession so it could be passed on to the poor and needy. Like many children I had terrible trouble finding something I didn't want to keep. I would shake my head at everything my mum suggested. Toys I hadn't played with for months would suddenly become my most prized possessions.

Eventually I'd offer a jigsaw with a missing piece or a book with the pages falling out, and Mum would get annoyed at me. She'd remind me how well off I was compared to the poor children receiving the toys, how they were probably orphans without loving homes to live in. I'd feel a bit guilty, and something would be decided upon, removed quickly by Mum, wrapped up and hidden away till the night of the procession.

On the night itself, we would watch the procession pass by. Lorries would be lit with Christmas lights, and people in fancy dress would hold out fishing nets into which we would drop loose change that would be collected to buy more presents. Then everyone gathered at the Market square in the town centre to sing carols.

When the evening finished, Dad would buy us all chips from the best chip shop in town. He'd add vinegar and sprinkle salt, and I'd feel the heat on my fingers as he placed a bag in my hands. The night was almost always a cold one, and walking home through the soon-to-be Christmas streets, the chips would give us inner warmth as we ate.

In the 1950s Christmas time didn't start at the end of the summer, as it does now. It crept up on us slowly, unbelievably slowly. It was as if something was holding back the days, as if the days had lead weights attached to them. Something, it seemed, was delaying the hands of the clock, preventing them from turning. The distance between waking and bedtime often seemed like an immense gulf that would prove impossible to fill.

'I'm bored,' I would announce. I didn't want to play with my old toys. I was anticipating all the new ones I'd be playing with on Christmas Day. I would wander from room to room, wondering what I might find to kill the boredom. 'Fill up a scrapbook,' Mum would suggest. 'Read a book, tidy your toy cupboard, get rid of a few things so there'll be room for anything new you might have at Christmas.'

Christmas Eve was worst of all: an infinite chasm of a day that stretched eternally ahead. I would be so bored that I'd even ask my mum if she needed any help. But Mum would spend most of the day baking – trays of mince pies, sausage rolls, jam tarts – and I'd just be in the way. The dog was no fun either. Attracted by the wonderful smells of home-made cooking drifting from the kitchen, Chum would wait around for any scraps that might fall to the floor. How that dog could eagerly scoff raw pastry just didn't make sense.

Chum, being part spaniel and part Labrador, had the Labrador 'look'. He would fix his big sorrowful eyes on Mum and she'd be powerless to resist. Bits of sausage meat would suddenly find their way into his mouth, and he'd do it all the more. In his doggy brain, giving Mum sorrowful looks equalled titbits to eat. Wherever he sat himself, and whoever he stared at, he was rarely disappointed. But despite his huge intake of food, his weight never seemed to change too much, as he always had a couple of walks each day to chase around with other dogs.

Christmas Eve was the time when we met up to swap gifts with other members of the family. We would set off loaded down with presents and call in on Dad's brother Jack and his family. Mum would be persuaded to have a small sherry to drink while Dad, because of his diabetes, would maybe have a tiny drop just to be sociable. If I was lucky I might be offered a Coke or a cherryade, rather than the dreaded orange squash, which I wasn't at all keen on. Once presents were exchanged, I would be allowed to open mine, which was strange, as these gifts seemed to have bypassed Father Christmas completely!

Later we'd move on to my dad's parents, where more gifts would be exchanged. Sometimes we'd have a meal there, all seated around a table that had been in the family for generations. Other aunts, uncles and cousins would appear and, by the time we went home to bed, it was late and my parents thought that I'd be sleepy. But I would be way too excited to sleep. Next day was Christmas Day. Really, it was so late it was almost Christmas Day already. I wouldn't be able to sleep, I knew it.

And so it proved. I tossed and turned, pulled off the blankets then pulled them back again, asked Mum for a drink, got told off, just couldn't get comfortable. And my mind was spinning. I was thinking of all the presents I'd asked for and the fun I'd have playing with them. Would the night ever end? Lying in my bed was like being trapped in sticky tar, unable to free myself from its grip. The night just wouldn't let go of me. 'Count sheep,' my mum would advise, or in exasperation, 'Count reindeer!'

Somewhere along the way though, I would fall asleep. But I'd always wake up early. One Christmas I woke up when it was still dark, shone my torch and found that Father Christmas had been. There was a tantalising sack of presents at the foot of my bed. I tried to get back to sleep but I couldn't. When I looked at the clock it said half past four. Surely that wasn't too early to open my presents.

I sneaked into Mum and Dad's bedroom and touched

my dad's shoulder. He woke and peered at me.

'Dad, it's Christmas Day. Can I open my presents?'

My Dad reached for his glasses on the bedside table. 'What time is it?' he asked sleepily. I picked up his clock and showed him. He groaned. 'It's half-past five, I suppose we'd better let you. We won't get any peace if we don't.'

I couldn't believe my luck. In his sleepy state my dad had read the time wrongly. If I told him the actual time I'd certainly be sent right back to bed.

I kept quiet. I dragged my sack of presents into Mum and Dad's room, climbed in to bed between them and began tearing off the paper from my first present. It took half an hour or so to open everything, and I don't remember either my dad or my mum joining in with much enthusiasm. After waiting hours for me to actually get to sleep so they could put the sack in my room, they'd probably only had three hours sleep at the most, but I didn't care. Whenever their eyes began to close, I would nudge them to look at another present.

When I'd finally finished my dad looked at the clock again. He shook it, then looked again. 'I thought you said it was five-thirty when you came in an hour ago?'

'You said it was five thirty, Dad,' I said. 'You must have been mistaken.'

'I *was* mistaken,' my dad said, 'to let you open your presents at such a ridiculously early time. Now go back to bed,' he ordered. 'And don't disturb us again till seven o'clock.' I did as I was told. But I didn't think singing the last verse of *O Come All Ye Faithful*, the one that's only meant to be sung on Christmas Day, would count as a disturbance. I thought that, with Dad being religious, he would appreciate my enthusiasm. He didn't. And *I* didn't think that, 'Brian, will you belt up?' was a very festive response!

There would always be a special breakfast on Christmas Day: home-cooked ham and eggs. Wonderful. Then time to play before Nan arrived along with her brother Horace. These two seemed to enjoy playing games with me, and it wouldn't be long before they were trailing round the room being coaches in a train or Indians in my game of cowboys.

My mum always served up a fantastic Christmas lunch. It was before turkey became the favourite choice, so chicken was generally the meat, although I do remember one year eating rabbit, along with sausages, bacon, stuffing and all the vegetables that Dad had grown in our garden. Dad had a particular liking for sprouts and Mum always cooked a saucepan full of them. I really couldn't understand how anyone could eat sprouts with any enthusiasm whatsoever. They smelt awful, and when they were being cooked, the smell seemed to spread through the house. It always reminded me of the smells that Chum produced when he'd eaten something nasty he'd found in the fields. 'If he's not rotten, he's dead ripe' was something my mum used to say when she caught a whiff of one of Chum's unpleasant fragrances.

'Afters' – my mum's word for sweet – was Christmas Pudding into which she slotted several silver sixpences for luck. Not so lucky if you bit into the pudding and cracked a tooth, or let the slippery coin slide down your throat!

Dad, having served in World War Two, was fond of telling stories about the places he'd eaten Christmas dinner whilst abroad, particularly the one about eating off the bonnet of an army lorry in Austria.

After lunch we would always watch the Queen give her speech. If I made a noise, Nan would be quick to remind me about children in her day being 'seen, but not heard.'

Then we'd play games, often Monopoly, with me the unscrupulous business man out to cheat my way to victory.

In the evening the aunts would arrive: my dad's sisters, Doris and Nellie, and his brother, Jack, with his wife, Olive, plus my older cousins, David and Sue, Barbara and Christopher. They came to us because my mum had a piano in the front room, and both Nellie and Doris would play it. Dad loved a singsong, and as well as all the Christmas carols, there'd be songs from the war such as *We'll Meet Again* and *White Cliffs of Dover* and even older tunes such as *If You Were the Only Girl in the World*,

It's a Long Way to Tipperary and one about a girl called Daisy on a bicycle made for two. My dad had a good voice and would lead the singing with great enthusiasm.

There would be games too: quizzes that Dad had made up like Guess the Advert, or charades, or we'd play pin the tail on the donkey. To do this you'd be blindfolded and given a tail with a pin in it. On the wall would be a picture of a donkey that someone had drawn. The donkey would have no tail, and whoever was blindfolded had to move towards the picture and pin the tail where they thought the tail should go. The results were often hilarious.

Later in the evening Mum would bring out all the mince pies, jam tarts and sausage rolls that she'd baked on Christmas Eve, and there would be crackers and nuts and more songs at the piano till Christmas Day turned into Boxing Day and everyone went home.

By this time I would usually be asleep on the settee, and Dad would carry me up to bed. I'd sometimes wake to hear Mum call out, 'Harry, you've still got your hat on.' And looking up drowsily at my dad's face, I'd see that the pink or green or purple paper hat from a cracker would still be perched on his head.

Mum would be left to clear everything up. But she wasn't alone. Chum would be there, scoffing anything that had been left on plates and slurping at the dregs of people's drinks. I always wondered if he had a hangover the next day.

— CHAPTER THIRTEEN —

You'll Catch Your Death

I'm not sure whether winters were colder when I was a boy or whether I just think they were. We had no central heating in our house and relied on coal fires for our warmth. While I was in the living room where the fire was alight, it was reasonably warm, although the room always had cold spots where the fire never seemed to reach. My dad used to get so frantic about keeping the warmth in – he was always telling me to shut the door.

'Were you born in a barn!' he'd yell out, or 'Put the wood in the hole!'

In the evening we would all pull our chairs up close to the fire, Chum would be there first, sprawled out on the carpet. Sitting so close to the fire could prove dangerous if the coal wasn't as pure as it should be. There would be loud explosions, and burning pieces of coal would shoot out from the flames. Some would land on the carpet and need removing speedily before they burnt a hole. Others would land on Chum and be flicked away by Mum. There was always a smell of singed hair in the room, but Chum hardly seemed to notice. When Mum lit the fire first thing in the morning, Chum would move so close to the flames that he would singe his whiskers, which would send him skittering round the room, puffing and blowing until he was sure that the danger had passed.

Coal was delivered to our house by the coalman. Ours was called Bill. Each delivery meant that Bill would carry ten or twelve sacks of coal, one at a time, from his lorry, though our front garden, along the side of our house to the coal bunker at the back, where he'd tip the sack up and the coal would rattle down. I felt sorry for him. His back was always bent from the coal he carried. It seemed a particularly unpleasant way to earn a living.

On one occasion I remember a coal ship getting into difficulties off the coast. To try to keep it afloat, most of the coal was dropped overboard. 'We'll be looking out for that,' Dad said.

He knew that anything that fell from ships might well be washed ashore on the beach. He'd picked up timber before, brought it home, dried it out, and made good use of it. So each day after the news he looked out at the beach for the first sign of black patches, ready with his bucket for when they appeared. We ended up with quite a bit of free coal that week, but Mum finally banned Dad from bringing home any more of the wretched stuff after the night where we all had to crouch behind the settee while the coal crackled and spat like rounds of gunfire.

But it was cold in our house, particularly when snow was on the ground. I really do think that Eskimos would have felt at home with us, or a colony of penguins. A polar bear could have lived quite happily in the cupboard under our stairs.

I never wanted to go to bed, because it meant leaving the fireside and heading off to the frozen wastes of my bedroom. I'd be clutching a hot water bottle which Mum had made for me, a rubber bottle that she would fill with boiling water before sealing it with a stopper.

On really cold nights I'd beg for a second bottle so I could hold one against my back with the other at my feet. I'd wear bed socks too, ones my mum had knitted, and thick pyjamas. On top of me would be several blankets and an eiderdown (like a thin duvet but nowhere near as warm).

Because of all the stuff I'd piled on top of me, I would usually get too hot in the night and wake up sweating. Off would come the socks, out would go the water bottles, and I'd be flapping the sheet trying to cool myself down.

Waking in the morning, I'd find ice on the inside of my windows and see my breath in the air. I'd snuggle down beneath the covers, and it would take all sorts of threats before Mum could get me out of bed.

There were no fitted carpets anywhere in my house, so getting out of bed was a risky business. If the rug slid away, then my bare feet would touch cold floorboards and I'd be doing some strange kind of war dance that took me across the room and into my slippers.

Taking a bath in this kind of weather was again something to be avoided. We had a small electric heater high up on the bathroom wall, but it barely made any difference. Dad would light a paraffin heater before he had a bath, and the bathroom would fill with a ghastly smell. He didn't seem to mind it but it wasn't for me. My baths were lightning quick.

In the 1950s most houses and streets were still lit by gas stored in giant gas holders (gasometers). These were cylindrical tanks that rose up from the ground. They rose higher as more gas was added to them, and then sank down again as the gas was used up. The gas works were just a few streets away from where we lived in Ramsgate.

We passed them each day on our route to the town centre, and this big industrial complex always seemed quite out of place in our seaside town.

The gas itself was made from burning coal, and everyday coal would be brought to the works in lorries or even horse and carts. In World War Two, the gas works were bombed and 'runaway' gas leaked into the sewers, where it exploded beneath a nearby house, knocking a man in the garden off his feet.

I hated the gas works. I hated the way they steamed and hissed and rumbled as we passed by. On one side of the road was a huge metal grating set into the pavement. You had to walk over this to get past, and at unexpected intervals a warm blast of air would funnel up from below. Whatever it was, and wherever it came from, the smell was awful. It reeked of death and decay, of the tideline sewage, and once it got up your nose and into your lungs, it stayed with you no matter how much you coughed and sneezed and tried to rid yourself of it. In a famous fifties film, an actress called Marilyn Monroe was filmed standing over a grating while air from below lifted her skirt all around her as she tried to hold it down. Whatever was being pumped from below on that occasion, it certainly couldn't have come from the gas works, or Marilyn would have fled the scene immediately!

Quite often the gates of the gas works were open and passers-by could see the confusion within. It seemed that the gas works sucked in men, men with hair bleached white from the gassy atmosphere, who slipped between the sizzling, scalding pipes with death defying steps. We would watch them stoke the fires with coal, shovelling it into huge boilers, supplying them with the fuel they needed to produce the gas. It seemed to me that somewhere in all of this fire and steam, in these nightmare flames, this hellish inferno, the Devil himself surely sat and gloated.

From the gas works' chimneys, clouds of steam issued forth and floated into the sky. For some strange reason, I'd stand and watch, picking out shapes in the steam. I'd give them names too, the names of our relatives – that's Uncle Horace, and that's Auntie Doris, and that's Mum, and that small one, that's me! It kept me amused, and I loved the way they lazily drifted through the sky, heading to somewhere I couldn't go.

I think I might have had the thought that everyone becomes clouds eventually, and that we follow each other all the way to paradise.

My mum always associated being cold or getting wet with catching colds. If I ever came home from school soaking wet, she'd hurry me indoors and tell me to get out of my wet clothes at once or I'd 'catch my death'. This was a favourite saying of hers. If I went outdoors in cold weather without a coat, I'd catch my death. If there was a cold wind I'd catch my death. If I sat in drafts, I'd catch my death. Maybe because she'd been so worried about me when I had pneumonia, she thought she was justified in 'mollycoddling' me. That was another word I heard from her. She was over-protective of me for much of my childhood. She would advise me about wearing a vest to soak up sweat in warm weather, or putting my jumper back on if I'd run around and got hot, so that I wouldn't then get cold and catch a chill.

The winter of 1963 was the winter of all winters for advice. Snow was on the ground from Boxing Day 1962 through to early March 1963. The newspapers called it, 'The Winter to End All Winters' and 'The Big Freeze'. 'Snowed to a Standstill' ran one headline.

To begin with, snow on Boxing Day was fun. Everyone was out building snowmen, sliding down the hill on toboggans, tea trays or sacks. I looked on enviously. No way were my mum and dad about to join in. Dad promised we'd go to the park in the afternoon so I could slide on the slopes, but the snow came down so heavily that our planned trip was abandoned.

The snow was still around at New Year's Eve. 'It's waiting for more to arrive,' my mother would say. And more did arrive. For the next few days blizzard followed blizzard. The snow formed huge drifts. Dad talked about 1947, when he'd experienced a similar winter, and we all wondered how long it would go on for. In some parts of the country there were snow drifts that were five metres high or more. Hundreds of villages were cut off for weeks with no one able to reach them.

Despite all the snow, I don't remember my school being closed. Health and safety wasn't given much priority in the 1960s, and both pupils and teachers were expected to struggle in as best they could. I was fortunate as I lived close to my school, but others had to catch the bus from Margate, or be driven in by their parents. They must have had some hair-raising experiences on the slippery roads! One thing I do remember is that one snowy lunchtime several of us nipped out of school and trudged round to the girls' school, where we successfully bombarded several girls with snowballs. It was, however, all over far too soon for our liking, as the shrieking and screaming from our unhappy victims soon caught the attention of the teachers, who warned that they'd ring our school and complain if we didn't disappear. So we did.

One of the things we enjoyed doing most in the snow was making slides. Again, these days salt would be strewn around before anyone could even think of sliding, but when I was at school, we used to get there extra early so that we'd have time to make one before the school bell called us inside. Everyone seemed to have a different way of sliding. Some boys crouched down, maybe with the thought that they'd have less distance to fall, others, far more acrobatic, ran onto the slide and managed to twist round and go down backwards. One or two decided that if here was a chance that they'd end up on their bottoms, it made sense to start off that way and treat it like a bobsleigh run. I remember once how Mr Hardy, one of our teachers at secondary school, borrowed a sledge and gave it a go, handing his bag to someone then speeding along to cheers from us all. It was amazing no one ever twisted an ankle or broke a leg.

At one point, that winter of '63, even the sea froze, between the two piers of Ramsgate Harbour. There were a couple of days when it was really possible to walk on water. Many people did it too, starting from one pier, then slipping and sliding over the ice, between trapped fishing boats, till they finally reached the other side. Dad wouldn't do it, and he wouldn't allow me to either. I couldn't swim, he reminded me, and that was that. Not that I would be doing much swimming if I fell through the ice. It was so freezing cold that I'd be an instant ice cube bobbing about in the water – in that situation my mum's 'You'll catch your death' would probably have proved true.

But it must have seemed dream-like, sliding along on the ice, a pale glow from a watery sun above, and a nightmare depth of sea beneath.

They'd been used to this sort of thing three hundred

years ago when the River Thames in London regularly froze over. They had frost fairs on the ice with carnivals, dancing bears, jesters and jokers all threading their way between the stalls. How I would have loved to have seen it all.

— CHAPTER FOURTEEN—

It's Them Kids Again

One more day of school,
one more day of sorrow,
one more day of this old dump
and we'll be home tomorrow.

When the summer holidays came round, we would play outside in the street every day. Those days there were far fewer cars around to interrupt our games of street football. Goals were chalked on garden walls or decided as being between the drainpipe and a pile of coats. We played across the width of the street, and amazingly there were very few accidents, and we managed to keep the ball clear of windows.

Most people were pretty good to us. If our ball went into someone's garden, we always knocked on the door and asked if we could get it back. But in the next street to ours, where one of my mates lived, and where we sometimes played, there was a garden we tried to avoid. If our ball was kicked in there, we would argue for ages about who should go and get it back. Usually it would end up being the one who kicked the ball, but if he was called away for his tea, then someone else would have to fetch it out.

The owner of the house was an elderly gentleman, a bad temper on two legs who made it very clear that he hated small boys. He particularly hated small boys who kicked their football into his flowers. It was no use asking nicely as this would simply alert him to the fact that there was a football in his garden. He would then pick up a garden fork positioned nearby and stab the ball with it. These balls had to be retrieved with stealth.

On one occasion, when it was my turn to risk his wrath, I had heaved myself up and over his fence, and was halfway to the ball when something told me I hadn't gone unnoticed. I must have triggered some garden alarm as, the next thing I knew, this guy was thundering towards me.

'I'll skin you alive,' he shouted out. 'I'll knock your block off! I'll tan your hide!'

None of this sounded particularly inviting, and with one last sprint I grabbed the ball. But before I could turn and make my escape I went down to the kind of tackle you would usually see at rugby internationals. Fortunately, such a performance at his age left him winded, crouched on the ground holding his stomach.

I crawled away, got to my feet and sprinted for the fence. Once back in the safety of the street, I turned and offered him some advice: 'You'll give yourself a heart attack.'

Recovering a little, he glared back at me. 'Next time,' he called, 'I'll be ringing the police.'

We should have left him alone after that little outburst but, of course, we didn't. We threw everything we could find into his garden: windfall apples, slugs, a dead cat that we found in a nearby alleyway. We targeted his prize dahlias for special treatment and left a selection of garden gnomes on his lawn. We'd removed these from another house in the street, whose owners seemed to have succumbed to gnome mania. I'm not proud of it now I look back, but if he hadn't declared war on us, if he hadn't burst our footballs, then we might have given him an easier time.

When the football season ended and the evenings grew long and almost warm, when the forecasts carried no warning of rain and the TV showed Australian cricketers arriving in Britain or British cricketers arriving in Australia, it was then time to forget football and pick up our cricket bats. We would watch the cricket on TV all day, till stumps were drawn about 6.30pm, and then we would chalk stumps on the garden wall and ball by ball recreate the latest test match.

We would play the parts of our heroes, batsmen Ted Dexter and Colin Cowdrey, bowlers like fiery Freddie Trueman and Brian Stathan, and polished all rounders like Edrich and Basil Dolivera. The rules were clear: four runs if the ball hit the shed, six for the far fence and 'out' if it left the garden or sliced Dad's tulips.

Once I remember a marvellous shot that was followed by the sound of breaking glass three gardens away. We were astonished and aghast at the same time. There was a heated debate about what should be done. Certainly no one felt inclined to go ask for our ball back. In the end we left it, and a few days later the owner of the greenhouse we'd hit asked my dad if he knew anything about it. Fortunately he didn't because we'd all kept our mouths shut. For a while after that we thought it best to play in other gardens, although none of my friends had a garden as long as mine.

We would keep figures too, whizz kids with

notebooks, cricket mathematicians, totting up runs, highest scores, numbers of wickets. We'd play the parts of our heroes till the evening sun gave up the fight, the light grew dim and Mum came out to stop play.

On rainy days we played 'Owzthat!' This was a game for two to six players but could also be played alone. We played it with two cylindrical dice, both with six flattened faces. The first dice (the batting dice) was labelled one, two, three, four, six and 'owzthat'. The second dice (Umpire's dice) was labelled 'stumped', 'caught', 'bowled', 'not out', 'no ball' and 'LBW' (leg before wicket).

If I played this with my friend Paul, we would toss a coin to decide who would be England and who would be Australia. Then we'd make up scorecards and toss again to decide who batted first. We would roll the batting dice and record the runs until 'owzthat' came up. Then the second dice would be thrown. There were four chances of being 'out', and if one of these came up, then the batsman's innings was over and we moved on to the second batsman. The game continued until all the batsmen of one team were 'out'. Runs were added up, then it was the turn of the second team to bat. Whoever scored the most runs was the winner.

This game kept us occupied for hours and hours, and we had notebooks filled with the results of our fictitious test matches.

*

'It's them kids again!' This was something of a street motto, particularly when we played one of our favourite games, 'Knock Down Ginger.' This was a game played everywhere when I was young, and one which had various names – 'Knock and Run', 'Knock-a-Door, Run' and 'Ding Dong Ditch' among others.

The idea, of course, was to knock on someone's door, or ring their bell, and then run and hide, preferably in a spot where we could hide and watch the puzzled face of whoever opened the door. If we really wanted to wind someone up, we'd knock a second time. This would result in a lot of fist waving and angry shouts seemingly delivered to no one.

Those of us with some sort of death wish would then try for a third attempt, knowing full well that the house owner might well be waiting behind the door ready to fling it open and, like a mad bull looking for someone to gore, make a lunge at whoever had been causing such annoyance. We would be held fast and roared at, or shaken about till we felt dizzy. Then, they let us go; there'd be a further warning.

'I know your dad. I'll be round to see him later.'

That was always a worry for me. My dad seemed to know everyone in the street.

There were variations on the basic 'Knock Down Ginger' routine, and over the years we perfected them.

One was the multiple door knock, which would only work in a street of terraced houses where the front doors all opened up onto the pavement. This involved tying thread through a number of door knockers and then unravelling the thread till you'd reached a place of safety. If you'd chosen your thread well, it would be thin enough so that it was hard to spot, but strong enough to yank and hear the satisfying knocks of the door knockers. Doors would open and the owners exit onto the pavement, and there would be much angry talking about what could be done about 'those flamin' kids.'

An alternative, which worked well in a street where terraced houses ran down both sides, was to tie thread to one door knocker, take it across the street and tie to the knocker of the opposite house. Then a tug on the thread before running for cover would see both doors opening and two people looking bemused at each other across the street. But the real crowning glory was if someone walking down the street failed to see the thread and walked into it, lifting the knockers on both doors. Then the two occupants of the houses would glare at the unfortunate passer-by, who would be very embarrassed by the whole thing. It was often impossible to control our laughter on these occasions, and the trees and bushes of the street would shake with our guffaws.

(Please don't try this today as it could be very dangerous for cars. There were hardly any on our street when I was a boy.)

In streets where there were front gardens, we'd dare ourselves to scoot up a long garden path, ring the bell, then scoot back down again before the door opened. There were accidents at times. My best mate Paul collided with a ladder as he was making his escape. It toppled over and flattened a hedge. Another friend, Les, backed away into somebody's ornamental fish pond and had to be hauled out by the angry owner of the house while the rest of us were just out of sight and laughing fit to burst! On another occasion I ran into an army of garden gnomes, sending them spinning like skittles.

Once we knocked on a door that we hadn't tried the trick on before. We ran to hide as usual but nothing happened. Slowly we emerged from our hiding places but the door remained shut. For some reason we crept closer and listened. We heard the sound of bolts being pulled back and a key being turned in the lock. Then a voice came from the other side of the door, a wheezy, crackly voice: 'I'm coming, I'm coming.'

Slowly the door creaked open to reveal a frail, very elderly lady. It would have taken all her strength to struggle up from her seat. We couldn't just disappear. She smiled at us and we apologised for disturbing her, but she said that we shouldn't worry about it. She was glad to see someone. She invited us in and we helped her back to her chair. We even made her a cup of tea. She told us where there was a tin with a cake in it. The cake didn't look too appetising but we didn't like to refuse. We told her that we'd call again, but we never did.

Every now and then there'd be a letter through our door telling us to move our cars, as the local council had decided that the surface of our road needed new tar. We didn't have a car so this didn't concern us, but there always seemed to be an odd vehicle or two remaining when the day came for the tar to be laid down. Often it was one that had been abandoned or that was permanently propped up on bricks and waiting to be fixed. Men from the council came with tow trucks and removed them. Then the fun could begin.

We would be out on the pavement watching as a massive piece of machinery rumbled and clanked into our street. It seemed to us as if it was as huge as an ocean liner, and it smelt as horrid as Hell. Flames would belch out from beneath it as the tar poured out of its belly. Following on behind would be a steam roller flattening the tar to make a road surface. This would then be attended to by six men with broom handles. On the end of the handles were fixed flat pieces of wood which the men would use to stamp down the edges of the tar where it met the kerb.

The council always seemed to choose one of the hottest days in summer to do this job, and the tar would stay sticky for ages. This was wonderful for kids like us. There were lots of ways that you could fool around with sticky tar. We would pick at it with lolly sticks, then flick it at each other. We would smear it on telegraph poles so that anyone who brushed against them would feel its sticky pull. We spooned it onto the pavement, then wrote our initials in it or played noughts and crosses. It made a terrible mess. Everyone picked it up on their shoes.

'It's them kids again,' we heard. 'Someone should give them a clout.'

In the 1950s lots of new houses were being built to replace those that had been destroyed in the war. On the weekends the half-built houses were abandoned by the builders, and we could sneak in and out of them as we liked. Winter days were good, when there was ice on the ground and frozen puddles. We'd pretend they were mirrors and smack down house bricks to crack the surface. My mum always claimed that you'd have seven years bad luck if you broke a mirror, but this way we had the fun without the worry.

Then there was pipe walking (like tightrope walking but a little easier). Or we would use a length of timber to make a seesaw, or balance on the edge of trenches while walking a line of bricks. It was a delicious feeling, knowing we were somewhere we shouldn't be, with no one around to tell us off. These days there would be security guards or CCTV to prevent anyone doing stuff like that.

One summer holiday we were all gripped by the desire to travel down the hill that I lived on at crazy speeds. To achieve this ambition, my mates and I needed to build some sort of vehicle. It so happened that another group of boys in a nearby road had built themselves a go-cart. It looked great fun and we couldn't wait to have one too.

We searched though our dads' sheds. Someone found an old pram and we ripped off the carriage and kept the wheels and axles. There was wood from a sledge, rope for steering, a large bolt so that we could connect the body of the cart to the steering mechanism, and a cushion for a seat. Somehow we made these bits and pieces into a go-cart, and we were ready for our test run.

We took it to the top of our hill and drew lots as to who would take the first run. Paul was the winner, although he didn't seem at all certain that this was any sort of privilege, and he climbed aboard and sat ready for the off. At the suggestion that we might push him, he almost jumped off. 'I'll do it myself,' he muttered, and slowly edged forward, hardly lifting his feet off the ground. I decided, at that point, that there was space for me to clamber onto the back of the cart, and despite Paul protesting that it was too dangerous, that is exactly what I did. There was nothing between either of us and breaking our necks but wooden brakes and a piece of flex that we'd tied to the front as a steering rope.

Our combined weight gave the cart extra speed and we were off. It felt really good to be racing along, but just short of where the hill met the road at the bottom of the slope, I suggested to Paul that it might be time to apply the brakes. This he did, but instead of doing it gradually, he slammed on the brakes all at once, and the cart tipped forward launching both of us into the air. Paul landed first with a cry of pain, while I came down on top of him then bounced off and slid along the pavement on my chin. Rubbing my chin I discovered a mixture of blood and gravel while Paul investigated how extensive the grazes were on his knees and elbows.

Despite warnings from parents that these carts could only lead to disaster, we carried on building them. The challenge was to build something that was bigger and more impressive than any of the others. Something that was sleek and shapely, that would tear down the hill in a blur of speed and was nifty enough to turn at the bottom of the hill and come to a cool, controlled halt. Sadly none of us had the foggiest idea how to do it.

My mum hated the thought of me being out on my go-cart, but Dad took pity on me and my feeble attempts and told Mum that if I couldn't be stopped then he'd make me something that was reasonably safe. He disappeared into his shed and assembled various bits and pieces. Later that week he brought other bits home from somewhere or other, and the next weekend we saw very little of him.

We heard lots of banging coming from the shed, and towards the evening he emerged with a cart that I knew would be the envy of the neighbourhood.

We took it to the top of the hill and I climbed aboard. It was brilliant. Off I went, with Dad keeping pace to begin with till I picked up speed.

'Brake slowly and in good time,' Dad called out.

That was something I had learnt from our previous mishap, and I managed to slow down to a smooth stop. Dad seemed delighted.

'That should keep him safe,' he reassured Mum.

And it did too. My cart had nothing to do with what eventually caused go-carts to be banned from our street. I was just doing what Dad had taught me.

By now the five of us who played together all had our own go-carts. Mine, of course, being built by my dad, was far superior in design and construction and in its safety features.

One morning we'd began our racing early and by 10 o'clock were whizzing down the hill, much to the annoyance of everyone who lived in the street and found they had to navigate a race track just to cross the road.

We would have been fine if we'd carried on with solo runs, waiting till one person reached the bottom before the next set off, but of course this got a bit boring and we thought we might liven things up a bit. I can't remember who suggested that we should all go down together. Maybe it was me, as I went in front to lead the way.

Once we were in a line, the signal was given to start and we set off. Concerned for the person behind, we were going much more slowly than usual, and everything would have been fine if an elderly lady on a bicycle hadn't suddenly appeared at the bottom of the hill and paused to speak with someone. We must have been about twenty metres from her. 'BRAKE!' I screamed.

My cart came to a smooth halt just a metre or so from the lady on the bike. I breathed a sigh of relief, but my relief was short-lived. Paul's cart smashed into the back of mine. The force from this collision was enough to propel me forward so that I then slammed into the lady's bike. The bike tilted and she fell with it. At that same moment Paul's cart was hit by the one behind him, again shunting him forward into the back of mine. This happened twice more, and by the time everyone had come to a halt, the lady and her bike had been pushed across the road and both were almost on the opposite pavement. One of her bike wheels looked buckled, while the other was spinning round. The lady was on the ground beneath her bike. She was lying still, and my first, horrific, thought was that we'd killed her.

The commotion had alerted people in the corner shop,

who ran out and helped to lift the bike and free the elderly lady. We didn't know what to do. Our faces were white as we realised the enormity of what we'd done. I can hardly describe my relief when we heard the lady speaking. She wasn't dead, but she was obviously very shocked. She was taken into the shop and sat down while someone made her sweet tea. Fortunately she'd fallen on her bottom, so there were no broken arms or legs.

My mates and I decided that we should try to apologise, and amid glares from everyone else in the shop, this is what we did.

She was sweetness itself – no telling-off, nothing. 'Boys will be boys' was what she said. 'I'm sure you didn't mean it to happen.' I remember us backing away, muttering our apologies again and thanking her for her kindness. I think perhaps we even bowed, so grateful were we that she'd suffered no serious injuries and was able to be so understanding.

But our go-carting days were over. We knew that. Our dads took the go-carts and broke them up. I think that Dad must have suffered a bit of aggro from Mum for being so silly as to build me a cart, but fortunately she soon forgave him.

There were times in the summer holidays when my mates were away from Ramsgate, either on holiday with their families or visiting relatives. I'd mooch around looking for something to do and someone to do it with. There were two brothers who lived in the next road to mine, and my mum used to warn me against playing with them. It was rumoured they never washed – you could see the tidelines of grime on their necks. They swore and smoked, picked up cigarette butts in the street and recycled the good tobacco in their own homemade cigarettes. They lived with their dad, and it was said that their behaviour had driven their mum away. When I asked where she'd gone, my mum always replied 'Chartham'.

Chartham was a place where there was a hostel for women who had nervous breakdowns. Occasionally, when I'd done something I shouldn't, or when I'd been particularly annoying, she'd say, 'Carry on like this and I'll be in Chartham.' That worried me. I certainly didn't want that to happen.

So for most of the time I kept clear of Jimmy and Jonny. They really weren't the sort of boys who encouraged you to go near them. Stories were told of how they picked up dogs' muck and threw it at each other or at anyone who happened to pass by. You certainly never wanted to play tag with them.

There was nothing in their garden. It looked like those pictures we'd seen of battlefields after the shelling. We held our noses as we hurried by, worried the smell was contagious. We never saw their dad without a fag in his mouth or a week's growth of stubble. A string vest covered his mighty chest. Coming home he'd call for his two 'little terrors', then wrap them in his huge tattooed arms and squeeze till they yelled for mercy. I wasn't supposed to play with Jimmy & Jonny, but I did!

Days were long in the summer holidays. Sometimes I'd leave the house with my bike soon after breakfast, pop back for lunch, and then be gone again till Dad came home for tea. I'd be with my mates at the recreation ground doing stunts on the swings and the roundabout, or fishing down at the harbour. There were no computer screens to peer into, hardly any television to watch in the day time and no mobile phones on which to ring, or be rung from, home. Parents trusted their children and trusted that we'd be safe. Had they known some of the things we got up to, they would have been worried sick. Our guardian angels were seldom off duty, but somehow we survived with our memories preserved.

Most days in spring and summer we would play out in the street until dusk, until mums started calling out, 'Time to come in' or 'Time for bed'. And in those final minutes before dads would be sent out to drag us in, there was always time for one more crack at the opposite goal, one last whack of bat on ball, one more call to the girl down the hill, 'He loves you, he does...' And in we'd race. There'd be trouble tomorrow, we thought, and there usually was.

CHAPTER FIFTEEN

Boredom Busters

'Childhood is full of long periods of utter boredom.'
– Aerony Ellis

Most of us were mad about collecting things: tea cards, stamps, comics, marbles. I had a huge collection of toy soldiers which Paul and I would use to play war games in my back garden. We would spend an hour or two arranging the soldiers into two different armies occupying two nearby flower beds. We'd dig trenches, build mounds, set up command posts among the bluebells and generally have a great time getting our hands and knees muddy.

Then the battle would begin. We'd take it in turns to throw clods of earth at each other's armies, destroying whole ranks of soldiers that we'd previously arranged in battle formations. Alternatively we'd each pretend to fly a model plane over the battlefield and drop bombs on the soldiers below. Such activities would be accompanied by suitable bomb-dropping noises as the missiles hit their targets. At the end of the battle the winner would be the one with the most toy soldiers still standing. Needless to say, my dad wasn't too keen on this game, as quite often his flowers became casualties of war!

Sometimes we'd play soldiers ourselves, using suitable tree branches as machine guns and *ack-ack-acking* our way round the garden. We had toy guns that were replicas of real ones and had names like 'Mustang', 'Colt 45' and 'Rodeo'. They fired caps – small amounts of gunpowder and a zinc alloy. These came in rolls of fifty or so, and the guns opened up to allow us to load a roll. As the trigger was pulled back the roll of caps would advance so that the first one was struck when the trigger was released, causing a small explosion and a puff of smoke.

My best gun was black with a white plastic grip, and I wore it in a holster attached to a belt around my waist. At night I often kept it under my pillow, just in case...

Occasionally Chum would be drawn into a garden battle and captured and held as a hostage by one of us.

The other would then try to mount a rescue. I would often hide with Chum in Dad's shed, although Chum generally failed to understand the need for secrecy and would wriggle back out into the open or give away our hiding place with a series of loud barks.

On other occasions we would move our activities to the streets, pretending we were stalking an invading army and picking them off one by one. Parked cars were used as cover. That is until enemy agents claiming to be the owners appeared and told us to clear off. We would quickly pull out the pin on an imaginary grenade and lob it in their direction before turning to run.

Dad had a wooden knife that he'd brought back from his wartime travels in Africa. He didn't like me playing with it, but often I'd smuggle it outside and make it part of my game. It was really a letter opener, but it looked real enough for us. He also had an army greatcoat, and on cold days I'd wear it even though it trailed along the floor behind me like a bizarre khaki bridal dress.

When we got bored of war, we'd try and hook things over the telegraph wires that ran the length of our street. Mostly we failed in our attempts, but occasionally we struck lucky, like the time Paul flicked a walking stick into the air and its handle hooked over the wire.

A few days later workmen appeared in the road with a vehicle that carried a large ladder. This was fixed at the base and could be extended skywards. One of the workmen climbed the ladder and unhooked the walking stick. We watched from our windows as the workmen looked round, trying to figure out who might have been responsible for hanging it there.

We kept things quiet for a while after that, till I got my kite tangled up in the wires. We imagined messages goobledygooked by the pull of the strings.

The workmen returned, stood around, stamped feet and considered what needed to be done. The wind had done a pretty good job tangling the kite, so when they finally got going, it took quite a time to unravel. Again the workmen looked round and glared. It was perfectly clear they'd had more than enough of our street.

Today, whenever I see a pair of laced together trainers that someone has managed to hang from the telegraph wires, I wonder why we never thought of doing that!

Another favourite was collecting car number plates.

Some boys preferred the railway station, where they could note down the number, make and model of every train that passed through Ramsgate, but that never appealed to me. However, I did fill page after page of a notebook with the letters and numbers of car number plates. Looking back, I'm not quite sure what I got out of it, but for a time I pursued this activity with a real passion.

A variation on the straight noting down of number

plates was to look for the letters that spelt words. Generally there were three letters and three numbers on number plates – something like AJD 694. Occasionally the letters would form a three letter word and these were fun to collect. Even my mum joined in with this game. We'd find words like 'run', 'cat', 'dog', 'beg', 'lip', 'leg', 'lot', 'pot', 'poo' and so on. It kept us amused, but probably doesn't seem a very exciting or worthwhile activity today!

My friends and I loved collecting autographs and competed to see who could get the most. Usually they were gathered from relatives or family friends, or from anyone we could catch leaving the stage door of Granville Theatre. But occasionally there'd be an actual celebrity. I remember queuing to get the signature of cricketer Godfrey Evans and showing it off to my mates. And once there was a Wild West Show in town, and I managed to get the autographs of several 'cowboys' who were lounging around outside. I was with Mum, and we were walking Chum. The cowboys started stroking Chum and calling him 'Hound Dawg' and 'Timber Wolf'. Chum lapped up all the attention, as he always did.

I asked Aunt Rose for her autograph, and she wrote at the front of my book:

If this book should ever roam,
box its ears and send it home to...

I then had to write in my address in case I ever lost it.

Someone else wrote their autograph right at the back of the book, with the words:

By hook or by crook I'll be last in this book.

Rainy days were Meccano days. Meccano were construction kits containing strips of metal that could be bolted together and combined with gears and wheels to make the most amazing working models: Tower Bridge with a platform you could raise or lower, a miniature Eiffel Tower or a working crane. Sadly, none of the models that I built ever looked like the one made by the beaming boy on the box lid. Mine were flawed in every possible way and often collapsed at the slightest touch. A career as an engineer was not for me.

As autumn came round each year, Conkers played a big part in our lives. All summer we would watch them grow on the trees, assessing which of the green spiky balls might hold champions. The best conker trees were in the park, and every year we looked forward to the annual battle between us and the park keeper. We would appear with half bricks, branches, Wellington boots, and throw them into the trees to try and bring down the conkers. The park keeper would come running, ranting and raving and threatening to call the police. Then he'd clamp his hands on our shoulders in a vice-like grip and steer us towards the gates. We would wait outside till he moved off and then sneak back in. We must have done a lot of damage to the trees. I remember the debris of leaves, twigs and broken branches that littered the ground – looking back, it must have been heartbreaking for the park keeper. But we were driven by a desire to find the champion conker that could defeat all others. Nothing else mattered and nobody could deter us.

Once we'd found a conker that looked as if it might be a potential champion, there were various ways we'd try to harden it. Some of my friends baked them in the oven for a short time. Others tried boiling them in vinegar or painting them with clear varnish. The conkers then had to have holes drilled in them so they could be hung on strings. There were often arguments as to the best way to drill a hole so that it would cause the least damage to the conker. My dad had a really sharp tool called a gimlet, which he used to make the hole for me. He wouldn't let me use it myself in case I spiked the gimlet through my hand. Then the string was attached with a knot at one end so the conker wouldn't slide off.

Conker contests were fought in the street or in the school playground. One player let his conker dangle on the string while his opponent swung his own at it. The idea was to cause the most damage to your adversary's conker as possible. Once the conkers had hit each other they would be inspected for cracks. The game went on with conkers being alternately held or hit until one was completely destroyed. A winning conker became a one-er, a two-er, a three-er, etc., depending on how many other conkers it had beaten.

So sad that these days many schools have banned conkers from the playground. Apparently bits of conker might fly off and hit contestants in the face or the eye. I think we coped OK with that in my childhood.

Following on from the conker season came Bonfire Night. We would be collecting wood for weeks before the big event, carrying it back from various parts of the town and storing it in our garden sheds. We would find it at the harbour where ships had offloaded wood and left broken bits lying on the quayside. We'd find it in the park after the first autumn gales had struck. Once we dragged back half a tree. It sat in the front garden for ages till Dad got fed up with it and helped us saw it up.

We'd buy the fireworks well in advance of Bonfire Night so we could show them to each other and anticipate the fun we'd have. Mum wouldn't let me keep them in the house, so they needed to be stored in Dad's shed. This was very wise, as Mum was fond of telling me about a family who had let their son keep his fireworks indoors. Apparently he'd been gazing at them lovingly (as I was prone to doing), but when called away had left the lid open on the box. A stray spark from the open fire then gave the family an indoor firework display that just about ruined every piece of furniture in the room. Apparently the family cat, which was sleeping by the fire at the time, was so freaked out by what happened that it left home and was never seen again!

In the week before November 5th we would make a Guy by stuffing an old pair of trousers with crumpled up newspaper, wrapping a jacket round a big bag full of more scrunched up newspaper, adding a football for the head, and tying on a plastic mask. If someone had a pram or an old go-cart, we would wheel the Guy out into the street and prop him up against a wall with a sign attached to him that read, 'Penny for the Guy'. The best location was just down the road from the corner shop, so that we could beg money from anyone entering or leaving. We never made a huge amount, and to be honest, most of our guys looked pretty awful, but it was fun for a few hours.

On Bonfire Night itself we'd usually gather in my garden, which was bigger than the gardens of my friends. Dad would set our Guy on the bonfire, tied to a wooden stake, and then light the fire. Then we'd start the fireworks. I remember one year when the fireworks had been left in the box while we played with sparklers. Unfortunately a stray spark must have fallen into the box, and the next thing we knew a jumping jack was up and at us! We staggered around while the firework jumped and crackled around our feet. After it had fizzled out, Dad went to close the box, but just as he did another firework took off, and then a third. I hadn't realised that Dad was such an agile dancer till I watched him jump and wriggle to escape the fireworks whizzing and spinning around his feet. Fortunately our unexpected firework display was out of doors and could do very little damage, but it was a bit of a waste of a good box of fireworks.

A few miles along the coast road out of Ramsgate was a fireworks factory. This was made up of fifty or so single sheds, and I wondered why they didn't just have one big building. Dad reminded me that when you're working with gunpowder, it was far safer to restrict any explosion to a small area rather than risk damaging a whole factory. For a while I wondered if working for Astra fireworks might be an interesting career prospect, but the thought of singed eyebrows made me reconsider.

I hate to admit it, but when I was a boy I had scant regard for small creatures in the house or garden. Like other boys my first reaction was often, 'What is it? Urggh! Kill it.' I look back on that now and feel both disgust and remorse. If I could undo what I did, I would do so immediately, but I can't, and I've lived all these years with these crimes on my conscience. I've tried to make amends. I've picked up worms that have strayed onto the pavement and placed them back in the grass. I've gently enticed small spiders from the bath and then given them their freedom. We've always had a spider catcher in the house for bigger beasts, who when caught have been offered a new start to life in the garden. I've caught mice in humane mouse traps, and when we kept chickens I even used a rat trap that imprisoned the rodents rather than snapped their spines. (Apparently rats won't return if you take them two miles away, so I regularly transported them to the other end of our village – the posh end – before giving them their freedom. I don't think they could quite believe their luck, and I'm sure, on one occasion, I heard one whisper 'sucker!')

But when I was younger, I wasn't so compassionate, and when my mates and I were bored, one activity we would get up to was to hold snail races. First off, there was the hunt to root out as many snails as we could from damp places around the garden. These would then be examined, and the active-looking ones separated from those we judged to be un-athletic. Looking back, how we made these distinctions, I'll never know. Then once we'd identified our possible gold medal winners, we would line them up on a starting line, sprinkle them with water to wake them up and then place bets on which would move furthest. Sometimes we'd paint numbers on their shells for easy identification.

Snail racing, however, wasn't something we could

really get excited about. It would take ages for the snails to wake up and actually get themselves into gear. Quite often they'd completely fail to understand what was expected of them and set off in the wrong direction. By this time we would have realised that we'd been far too optimistic about where we drew the finishing line, and the course would be shortened.

Finally one or two snails would start to slide along in approximately the right direction, and with the occasional reminder as to which direction they should be moving in, the race would be on.

We'd place a piece of cabbage or lettuce on the finishing line, hoping to encourage those snails within sight of the finish to maybe put on an extra spurt. But the races took so long that often we'd wandered off and found something more interesting to do by the time they got anywhere close.

Quite often Dad would come back from work to find the snails that we'd collected in a large group around the lettuce leaf. Unfortunately snails (and slugs) are the vegetable grower's nightmare. Dad would rant and rave, and we'd feel guilty as he picked them up threw them over the fence, back into the field where they had probably come from in the first place! He could never bring himself to stamp on them. I think he reckoned that this way they had a chance of survival. If their shells didn't crack on impact, a few would land on soft grass, and although probably dizzy from their flight (a somewhat unusual mode of transportation for a snail!), survive to tell the tale.

Caterpillars were an even bigger curse for Dad. He grew cabbages each year, and every caterpillar season would be out in the garden searching through the leaves. I would help him sometimes, particularly if he offered me money to do so. We'd pull off the caterpillars one by one and place them in a jam jar. They smelt disgusting. (A warning to anyone reading this: don't eat lots of cabbage or you'll smell like that too!) Once he had a large number, he would fill the jar with water and drown the pests.

I once found a giant caterpillar with beautiful markings, something totally alien to any species I'd encountered before. I kept him in a box covered with a lid and hid him away from my dad. Within the box I tried to create for him something close to the caterpillar's natural habitat. I used privet leaves and twigs, but he seemed unhappy, refusing to eat. One day he cocooned himself. He emerged about six weeks later, the ugliest moth I had ever seen.

After tea, when there was no one else to play with, I'd go out into the garden and look for earwigs. There was always an overflowing nest beneath the bird bath, and there were also loads to be found in holes in the concrete posts that held up our garden fence.

I would take hold of a garden cane and poke it into the holes, causing turmoil in their earwiggy lives. Then, with my eye to the hole, I'd watch them scuttle, wall of death-like, round and round, till they fountained out and fell to the ground or were safety-netted by flowers. There were casualties, of course, lives lost, small bodies squashed. I knew it was wrong, but something always pulled me back. It's something I now deeply regret.

Inside my mum's greenhouse I found a spider, a real King Kong spider, a spider the size of Godzilla. Each night he would build a web, but he didn't seem very good at catching things to eat. I decided to help him and filled his web with wasps and flies that I slaughtered each day. I saw him as some sort of Egyptian god who had enslaved me and was demanding daily sacrifices. He grew fatter and fatter and seemed genuinely pleased with his good fortune. To begin with, when I entered the greenhouse he would disappear to the edge of his web, but after a while he'd stay at the centre and pounce on the things I threw in. After a while my mum issued an ultimatum: I had to get rid of the spider or I'd be cooking my own tea. It was a no brainer. I had no idea how to cook, so the spider had to go. I caught him in a jar and relocated him in a rose bush. He can't have thought much of his new situation as the next day he was gone.

But some creatures eluded me. Across town were the chalk pits, an area of land next to the railway line where huge holes had been gouged into the chalk on which Ramsgate was built. There we would hunt for lizards. They say that if you catch a lizard by its tail, the tail will break off, allowing the lizard to escape. In time it would then grow a new tail. Sadly, I never once caught sight of a lizard, yet alone caught one, so I was never able to put this theory to the test.

CHAPTER SIXTEEN

Must Open Mouth & Speak Up

It was 1958. I was eight years and two months, and the first comment on my annual school report was, 'Must open mouth and speak up.'

It amuses me to think about it now, as since then I seem to have made a perfectly good living as both a teacher and a performance poet by opening my mouth and speaking up!

I did pretty averagely on that report. 'C' was an

average grade and I managed to achieve a C for every subject, apart from Craft, in which for some unknown reason I was given a B. I couldn't believe that. I've always been pretty useless at making things with my hands, and I was hopeless at woodwork in secondary school. My parents must have been a little disappointed that I didn't shine in my school reports, but school, for me, was a little dull.

I liked to write, but in English lessons there was seldom any free choice in subject matter. Our teacher would write three titles on the board, and we would have to choose between them for the subjects of the 'compositions' (stories) that we needed to write. One of them, I remember, was 'A Day in the Life of a Penny. How could anyone get excited about that?

Maths was called 'Arithmetic' or 'Sums', but whatever label it had, I wasn't very good at it. I was reasonably OK with numbers, but once they were disguised as problem solving, my mind was a blank.

So far, so average. But I must have done something right, because one day I was given a prize. I was nine years old, and I don't think the teachers could agree on what it should be for, so they gave it to me for perseverance. I wasn't sure what it meant. I didn't remember studying perseverance in our lessons. It was a mystery to me until Mum explained it. 'You've worked hard,' she said. 'They want to reward you for that.'

The prize was a book, and I was asked to write down the name of the one that I'd like. I had recently developed a real interest in reading, and as I was heavily (and I mean *heavily*) into Enid Blyton at the time, I wrote down the name of her newly published hardback book. It was three weeks to Prize Day, and my excitement increased with every day that passed. I loved the *Famous Five* books and dreamed of having adventures with Julian, George, Dick, Anne and Timmy the dog, investigating smugglers and secret tunnels, castles and spooky caves. But nothing too frightening. Enid got it right, of course: the Famous Five were far too clever for the bad guys, who always wound up arrested by the police.

I'd learnt to read with *Janet and John* books. These were books designed to get you reading through endless repetition of lines like 'Run dog run' and 'See the dog run'. They were so *boring*. I whipped through them as fast as I could, thinking that there surely must be something else to this reading game. And there was.

After what felt like forever, the day of the prize giving finally arrived. In just a few hours time I would have in my hands the book that I'd been wanting to read for ages. The morning's lessons dragged more than ever, but after lunch we all assembled in the school hall. Mrs Tyndall was on her feet, telling all the proud parents what a wonderful year we'd had. Then she introduced Wing Commander Hetherington, or whoever it was giving out the prizes, and the teachers began to get us in line so we could go on stage one by one as our names were called.

My turn came and I held out one hand for my book while the other was shaken vigorously by the Wing Commander. 'Well done,' he said and handed me my book. I took a look as I left the stage and immediately alarm bells started to ring. It didn't look like an Enid Blyton, and when I got back to my seat and examined it closely, I discovered that it definitely wasn't. I was devastated. There were no inviting pictures on the cover – it was just dark blue with letters embossed in gold that formed the words *Ivanhoe* by Sir Walter Scott.

However, all was not lost. *Ivanhoe* was a television programme that was all about knights and battles and swishing swords and rescuing damsels in distress. It might not be too bad. I opened the book and scanned the first page. Nothing in *Janet and John* had prepared me for the gobbledygook that met my eyes. It was unreadable. I recognised the odd word, but very little made any sense whatsoever. I realised later on that much of the book is written using Scottish words, as Sir Walter is a much loved Scottish writer, but to my childish eyes the book could have been written in Chinese.

'Keep it safe,' Dad said, 'You'll read it when you're older.' But that wasn't the point. I'd earned the book and I wanted a book to read right there and then.

I did as he told me and put the book away on a high

shelf. But, although many years later I still have it, I have never read it! It's hard to get over such disappointment. Mum realised that, and a couple of days later, she presented me with a package. I ripped it open and there it was: the prize I really wanted, the latest Blyton hardback book. It must have cost my parents a lot of money, but I was fortunate in that they both knew how important reading was to me, and still is.

My parents didn't read a huge amount themselves, although my mum bought a magazine each week and my dad had a collection of books that he dipped into now and then. I looked at his books occasionally. There was one that had an orange cover with a silhouette of a hanged man on its spine. It was a book with fifty ghost stories, and I really wanted to read them but was frightened that they might give me nightmares. Time and time again I picked up the book and dared myself to look inside it, but that's all I ever did. I never read a single story.

But I did read comics, lots of them. I read war comics in which the British army defeated the Germans on every occasion. I kidded myself that I could speak German, having learnt from these comics words such as 'Achtung' (Attention!), 'Hande Hoche' (Hands Up!) and 'Donner und Blitzen! (Thunder and Lightning!). I also read *The Beano*, for the adventures of Dennis the Menace and Minnie the Minx, and *The Dandy* for Desperate Dan and

Beryl the Peril.

Comics were fun because they sometimes contained free gifts. I remember toy submarines and divers which needed filling with baking powder. When placed in water they would sink to the bottom and then rise back up to the surface. Or there would be tiny bouncy balls or a stiff paper cracker that made a loud noise when flicked. None of the free gifts ever lasted very long, but the idea of having something for nothing was always an attractive one.

It was about that time that I began my lifelong love of libraries. There just weren't enough books around to satisfy my appetite. I'd got through the school reading programme so was able to choose whichever book I wanted, but the choice was limited. There were lots of easy versions of classic books such as *Treasure Island* and *Kidnapped*, books that had been written a hundred years or so ago, but I wanted books that were about children in today's world, books I could identify and engage with.

I read and read and read, beside the fire on cold winter evenings and under the bedclothes at night when I should have been going to sleep. Books hooked me; I always had my nose in one. However boring life was, a book could lead me away from everyday life and into fantasy worlds that would excite and inspire me. To my mind, a book was a ticket to an adventure, and that's something I'm always speaking about to the children I meet when I visit schools as a writer.

One day my mum took me along to the library and showed me the children's section. There were shelves full of books by Enid Blyton that I'd never read.

I joined Ramsgate library, and I've been a library member somewhere or other ever since. I carried home two books that day, and two days later I'd read them both. Back we went for two more. Once I'd finished with Enid Blyton, there was Jennings and his friend Darbishire, in a series of books by another wonderful writer called Anthony Buckeridge. They were set in a boys' prep school, and I was captured from the first one. The books were funny and Jennings was always in trouble, particularly with his form teacher Mr Wilkins, who was a man with little patience and a fiery temper.

I roamed the woods and built camps with William and the Outlaws, Henry, Ginger and Douglas, in the wonderful *Just William* books by Richmal Crompton. It was a boy's world that she described, although the gang were often bothered by Violet Elizabeth Bott, who demanded that she played with them otherwise she would, 'Thcream and thcream 'till I'm thick'. (No, those aren't spelling mistakes – it's how Crompton wrote it in the books!)

Next up were the Billy Bunter stories, written by Frank Richards. These were set at Greyfriars School, where Bunter was a pupil. Bunter was an unlikely hero in that he was stout, deceitful, lazy and a glutton for food. He would do anything he could for some grub, even if it meant helping himself to his classmates' cakes and sweets. Often this would result in him receiving 'a good kicking' once his crimes were discovered.

After I'd devoured all the Billy Bunter books that the library had to offer, I discovered the *Biggles* books by Capt. W.E. Johns. These were originally written for an older audience but appealed very much to young boys. Biggles was a fictional pilot who had flown in World War One and in the years that followed. Longing for such adventures ourselves, my friends and I would imagine ourselves sitting alongside Biggles in the cockpit of his plane while he shot down German air aces or battled criminals around the world.

In the late 1950s there were also libraries in Boots the Chemist, and they seemed to have different *Biggles* books to the ones I found in the Public Library. Odd to imagine, when we think about the shop today, that once Boots had a library. You could pick up some sun tan lotion for your holidays and a book for the train at the same place!

There were very few 'Young Adult' books around when I became a teenager, and by the age of fourteen I was reading books from the adult library. I think I should have been sixteen to enrol, but the library staff knew me from my regular visits, and with my mum's permission,

I was able to start a whole new reading adventure. I had a little guidance from the librarians, but very quickly I was out on my own. The library was a treasure chest for me to explore, and sometimes I'd find a gem. I read all the Sherlock Holmes books and then moved on to James Bond, although my dad rather disapproved of the Bond books.

It dismays me these days to hear of so many libraries all across the country being closed down by councils. Do they have any idea how important libraries are? Ramsgate library was burnt down a few years ago but has now been rebuilt and looks stunning. Whenever I go back to Ramsgate to visit my parents' grave, I always call in at the library to take a look around. That library made me a reader for life. I owe it a huge debt of gratitude.

All our work in the primary school was geared towards an exam in the final year called the 'Eleven Plus'. The results of this would decide which secondary school we went to. Those who did well would attend grammar school and receive an education that might hopefully lead on to university or college. Those who didn't would attend either a technical school or a secondary modern school, where the education would be geared towards making sure you found a job at the end of it.

There were three exams in the Eleven Plus: a) Arithmetic and Problem Solving b) English, including

Comprehension (answering questions about an extract from a book) and Composition, and c) General Knowledge.

Think back to the hardest test you've done. Well, it was like that, but worse. The pressure was enormous. Both teachers and parents ganged up on you, and extra homework was given to try to get you through to grammar school.

On the morning of the first exam I felt unwell. I think most of us did, apart from maybe the ones who'd already worked out that they hadn't got a snowball in Hell's chance and were just going along for the ride. I was so nervous I barely remember the exams themselves. What I do remember is the feeling of relief when they were over, followed by the long and anxious wait to find out how we'd done.

Results morning came round at last, and we waited nervously in the playground. Well, not all of us were nervous. Some were quietly confident that they'd done well. Others were bluffing us, telling everyone that they didn't want to go to a school where they'd have to work extra hard. I wanted to pass but was pretty sure that I hadn't done so. My maths would have let me down, I was sure, particularly the problem solving.

But a miracle happened that morning: I was told that I had passed. I think my teachers were surprised too. Looking back now, the only explanation I can think of was that I'd done OK on general knowledge. I'd learnt the dates of all the Kings and Queens from 1066 and can still remember most of them now. I knew most of the capital cities of the world, and maybe, just maybe, whoever marked the papers had seen something promising in my answers.

My mum and dad were overjoyed, but I was worried because, although my friend Richard had passed the exam, Paul and Andy had not. They tried to make out that they weren't worried, but I could tell how disappointed they were. That's what the Eleven Plus did, it split up friendships. It's always more difficult to keep a friendship going when you aren't at the same school.

CHAPTER SEVENTEEN

Is This A Hand Grenade?

Even though the war had finished five years before I was born, it was never far away from my childhood.

In World War One bombs had been dropped on Ramsgate with a huge loss of life, so with World War Two approaching, the Mayor of Ramsgate knew how important it would be to make sure the population of the town could be kept as safe as possible.

Ramsgate is just across the English Channel from

France, where the Germans were, and when German planes flew across the Channel to bomb London, Ramsgate often had bombs dropped on it too. Not that it was an important town, but if a German bomber was prevented from reaching London by English gunfire or by British fighter planes, the crew of the bomber would drop their bombs on any English towns they could before recrossing the Channel. They became known as 'hit and run' raids, and a lot of people lost their lives in them.

It was decided that a network of tunnels would be hollowed out of the chalk beneath Ramsgate and linked to a central tunnel which had previously brought the railway to the town's seafront. The network would be modelled on a tunnel system in the Spanish city of Barcelona, which had withstood some of the heaviest bombing in the Spanish Civil War a few years earlier.

Work started in the spring of 1939. The chalk on which Ramsgate is built was very easy to cut and needed no propping. The tunnels were deep, about sixty feet below the surface, and there were twenty-two entrances all around the town. They were completed and opened just before World War Two began. Once the Germans started their bombing raids in 1940, the tunnels saved hundreds of lives, particularly on one day when over five hundred bombs were dropped on Ramsgate in less than five minutes. 'Thank God for the new town shelters' was one resident's response.

My parents were both in Ramsgate at the start of the war in 1939. My dad was working in his father's furniture shop and my mother in a drapers (selling curtains, cloth, wool, buttons and so on).

My mother used to tell about the day she was in the High Street and German bombers suddenly appeared over the town. There had been no air raid warning, and bombs were already dropping close by. My mother was with a friend, who started running towards a butcher's shop. Butchers in those days had solid wooden benches where the meat was cut. You could crawl under them and probably be safe from everything except a direct hit. 'We can shelter in here,' she shouted to my mum.

My mum kept on running down the High Street to where she knew there was an entrance to the tunnel system. She stumbled down the steps and was pulled inside as the bombs fell behind her.

An hour later the All Clear sounded, telling people that it was safe to leave their shelters. My mum walked back up the High Street to find her friend in the butcher's shop. But there was no shop anymore; it had been flattened by a direct hit. My mum's friend had been killed in the attack. If my mum had made the wrong decision, she would have died too, and I wouldn't be writing this book. I used to regularly thank her for looking after me even before I was born.

The tunnel system soon developed into an

underground city as people left their homes and started living there. Huts were constructed from black sacking, large ones with double bunks for families and smaller ones for couples. Curtains were put up and meals were cooked on primus stoves.

The tunnels were shut up after the war, but we used to find ways of getting in, pulling down the barriers around the entrances and exploring beyond. They were terribly dangerous as there was rubble everywhere. There used to be regular falls of chalk too and flooding in wet weather. We could hear the drip, drip, drip of water seeping into the tunnels as we explored them. Whole expeditions would be mounted with torches to try to find wartime souvenirs and bring them out. My parents would not have been happy had they known.

I remember one afternoon, in the summer holidays, when Paul, Richard, Julian and I decided to go down and investigate. I'd found a map showing where the system went in relation to the streets above, and we wanted to see if we could enter the system through one entrance and exit where the tunnels came out in our school grounds.

Once in the tunnels and away from daylight, it was pitch black. The only light was from the torches we'd brought with us. There were steps and a rusty handrail leading down into deeper darkness, and we clung to this as we edged down the steps one at a time. There was loose chalk everywhere, and no one wanted a twisted ankle or a fall from a broken step.

In the darkness, it was hard to rid our heads of the ghost stories that were told about the tunnels. It was rumoured that a ghost train ran along tracks once used by the railway and that fireballs blew through the blackness. It was easy to scoff at these things in the daylight, but here, with only the faint beams of light from our torches to pick out the way, anything seemed possible.

At the bottom of the steps we turned a corner and found a further set of steps, narrower this time and again strewn with rubble. A tunnel led off from the steps, about two and a half metres high and a metre and a half wide. The torches threw our shadows onto the walls, long thin shadows like the ones you find in a Hall of Mirrors. The ground sloped downwards and soon we were splashing through water. At one point the water was up to our ankles, but we'd anticipated this and were all wearing Wellingtons.

Soon after this the tunnel divided into two. After a brief discussion we turned into the one that we thought most likely to lead towards our school grounds. But before long we stumbled into the remains of a rock fall, and we had to scramble up and over a heap of chalk. At one point there wasn't much room between the roof of the tunnel and the chalk pile, and we wondered whether we should carry on or abandon the trip. Something scuttled away in front of us and Paul's torch revealed a rat. Again we looked at each other. Where there was one rat, there would surely be more. Weren't rats dirty creatures, full of disease?

We moved forward, turned another corner and found the tunnel was dividing again. We took the left hand one, and then after a short stretch, another left hand turn, and continued till we suddenly came across some steps leading upwards. These were less tricky to climb and looked as if they'd recently been swept clear of rubble. After a while we saw daylight filtering through cracks in the walls and, peering though, we could see a large area of grass outside. We agreed that we must be approaching our school grounds. But there was no way out. The way was blocked by a huge concrete slab. It must have been recently sealed, as, when sneaking in from the other way, we'd always managed to squeeze past the brick work before. There was nothing for it but to return the way we'd come, if we could remember the way back.

As we descended back down the steps, I thought about the Greek Myth where Theseus, in search of the Minotaur in the labyrinth below Crete, unwinds a ball of thread as he explores the maze. He knew that by doing so he would be able to find his way out once the creature had been killed. Unfortunately a ball of thread had not been on the list of items we thought we'd need for the trip.

Just as we reached the foot of the steps, Richard

dropped his torch. The light went out and wouldn't come back on. 'Look, it should be simple enough,' I explained. 'We just need to reverse the turns we took earlier. We'll be fine. And we've still got two torches.'

We came across several falls of chalk, which we clambered over, found another blocked exit and sat on the steps eating the chocolate that we'd included in our supplies. I looked at the plan of the tunnel system that I'd brought with me and tried to relate where we were to the streets above, but it didn't make sense to me. We carried on and were dismayed to find that now the light from Julian's torch was weakening.

If it went completely, we would have one torch between the four of us.

I began to feel rather nervous, and could detect the worry in my friends' voices too. Would we be wandering around down here forever, going backwards and forwards, criss-crossing where we'd been before, still unable to find where we came in? I pictured four skeletons in the dust and thought of them being discovered in years to come by other tunnel explorers who had given more time and thought to their preparations. Then I told myself not to be so daft, we would be found long before then.

Nevertheless, it was eerie in the semi darkness, and with only the light from our last torch, we were all thinking what it would be like when there was no light at all. How would we cope? What would happen to us? We started searching again. After all there were twenty-two entrances to the tunnels and one of them must be an escape route.

Maybe we should stand at the top of the steps and shout to anyone passing by?

Up till now, the tunnels had been silent, apart from dripping water and the occasional scurrying of rats, but now we began to hear other sounds: the crunch of feet on the rubble, the echo of dislodged stones bouncing down the stairs. They seemed to be coming closer. The only explanation seemed to be that there was someone else in the tunnels apart from us. Soon we could hear voices too.

A little way back we'd come across a room that led off from the tunnel we were in, and we decided to turn around and go back there to hide. We turned off our torch and crouched down at the back of the room.

I was trembling, and wedged in tight against the others, I could feel that they were too. Together we'd become a quivering mass of jelly.

Loud footsteps were coming closer now. We hoped whoever it was would pass by. 'Hello,' a voice called, 'Is anybody there?' No way were we going to jump up and reveal ourselves, so we stayed quiet. It sounded like there were several people heading our way, and we heard what seemed like the crackle of a radio. A voice called, 'No sightings yet, but if they're here, we'll find them.'

Then the tunnel was lit up and light snaked into our

room to reveal our hiding place. 'Got them,' another voice called, and strong arms reached out and hauled us to our feet.

The firemen who had found us were obviously annoyed. We suffered a lecture about flaming kids causing them no end of trouble, and they marched us back to the entrance and took down our names and addresses. The police would be round later to see our parents, they told us.

We wondered how they'd known we were down there. One of the firemen explained that an old lady living nearby had seen us sneak into the tunnels. She'd been watching from her bedroom window, and after we didn't come out again, she'd been worried about us. She'd called the police, who had then called out the fire service. It was a regular occurrence, they said, and we'd better not do it again.

When I got home I admitted to my parents that we'd been down the tunnels. Neither of them were too pleased, and were even less so when a policeman called round to give me another warning.

Years later, when I was writing my children's novel *Python*, I decided to include the tunnels in the book. I contacted the fire service and asked if they still did regular inspections, and if so, would I be able to join them on one occasion as I needed to research the tunnels for my book. They agreed, and on one wonderful day I achieved two ambitions at once: I got to ride in a fire engine, and I went back down the tunnels legally! In 2014 the tunnels were finally opened to the public and guided tours can now be booked.

There were other reminders of war around the town, including a large amount of bomb sites where houses had been wrecked and not cleared away yet. They had become overgrown with weeds and grass, but they were still exciting play areas as you never knew what you might find there if you looked hard enough. We were always being warned of the dangers of unexploded bombs. These were bombs that the Germans had dropped during the war but which had failed to explode when they'd hit the ground. They were found quite often in our cities and towns and did sometimes explode when they were disturbed. Naturally my parents were concerned.

But boys, of course, can be both stubborn and foolish. We gave little thought to what might be lurking in the long grass. We regularly played football on a makeshift pitch in a cliff top park. Along one side of our pitch were railings. Beyond these was an area of rough ground covered with giant thistles, brambles and other bits of unpleasant vegetation. Then somewhere beyond this rough area was the cliff edge and a sheer drop of twenty metres or so to the beach below.

Every now and then some lad would boot the ball into

the rough ground between the railings and the cliff edge. He would be set upon by the rest of us in a fairly good-natured manner and then dragged to the railings. It was a rule amongst us that anyone losing the ball in this way had to go and get it back. No one wanted to climb the railings and then search for the ball, knowing full well that he might stumble upon something nasty in the nettles. When I think about it now, I feel sure that it must have all been checked for bombs, but we always fantasised that something might have been overlooked.

One or two lads refused to take part in this activity, and a kick into the rough ground would immediately see them running for their lives towards the park entrance, leaving the rest of us to draw lots as to who would be the one to fetch it out. One boy called Norman would often volunteer. I wasn't quite sure what he got out of this, because every time he dived into the undergrowth and threw the ball out, he'd struggle to get back over the railings. None of us waited to help him, of course, we just carried on with the game. Once, his braces snagged on the railings and he stayed there suspended like a puppet or a soft toy pegged on the line to dry. His limbs were jerking around and he twisted and turned as he vainly tried to free himself. But it was impossible. As soon as we realised what he'd done, the game stopped and we fell about laughing hysterically while he swore at us and continued with his wriggling. Finally we took pity on him, and before the braces could encircle his neck and throttle him, we helped him down.

Instead of being grateful for our help, he chased us round the park, picking up mud or dried dogs' muck and flinging it at us. Eventually, when he paused to collect more ammo, we charged him, knocked him down and then sat on him till he agreed to a truce. He was then marched to the park toilets while we checked that he washed his hands thoroughly before getting them anywhere near the rest of us.

But although none of us ever did end up being blown up on that clifftop, there was an occasion where I did find an actual relic of the war. I must have been ten or eleven years old, and I'd cycled down to the beach to explore the rock pools. I loved the beach and the slimy, slippery rocks that were revealed at low tide. On a rocky platform that stretched at the base of the cliffs for a mile or so along the beach, there were pools of water where all sorts of sea creatures could be found – crabs, starfish, jellyfish – all stranded until the sea returned.

I must have been rock-pooling for an hour or so when I saw something quite unusual. It was rounded metal, rusty and solid. I dug round it with my fingers till I was able to prise it from the sand. If I wasn't very much mistaken, it was a hand grenade. I'd seen pictures of them in the war comics I read, and this certainly seemed the right shape and size.

I should have left it where it was, but, of course, I didn't. Holding it carefully in my hand, I moved cautiously over the rocks to the beach and then up onto the promenade. Standing nearby, gazing out to sea, was an elderly gentleman who, to my mind, looked as if he'd probably seen action in one war or another. I went up to him and politely asked if I could show him something. He looked down at what was in my hands.

'Is this a hand grenade?'

This man was elderly, but his reactions couldn't have been quicker. He moved away from me with the speed of a turbo charged cheetah. He waved his stick at me and yelled from a distance, 'Don't drop it, whatever you do!' I was so startled that I almost did drop it.

'What shall I do with it?'

'Take it and hide it somewhere,' he shouted. 'Then tell the police.' He walked off briskly, obviously wanting nothing else to do with me or the possibly lethal object that I still held in my hands.

I found a small opening in the cliff face and tucked the grenade inside it, hoping that no one would find it before the police did.

When I got home my dad told the police what I'd found. He and I cycled back down to the beach and showed a policeman on a motorcycle where I'd hidden it. The policeman had a basket on the back of his motorbike and from it took out towels and blankets.

Gingerly he collected the grenade, wrapped it up in several layers and eased it into his basket. That was it, I thought, till the following week, when dad read out a small piece from the local paper. It said that a boy had found a grenade on the beach and that it had been taken away and detonated safely in a controlled explosion. I wasn't sure how you controlled an explosion, but was mighty glad that it hadn't exploded when I had hold of it!

Another relic of the war was in our back garden. Our house was one of three built on a bombsite. The rubble from the bombed houses had been cleared away and three new houses built. In the gardens behind the houses there were Anderson shelters left over from the war.

These shelters were made by digging a hole in the ground and then covering it with an arch of corrugated iron. Soil was then spread on top of the arch so vegetables could be grown. Sheltering in one of these must have felt a bit like being in a tomb. As they were underground, they were also full of water for much of the time and would need constant baling out as the bombs fell all around!

Dad decided to keep his shelter, construct wooden sides, raise the roof, give it a door and, hey presto, he had a shed! Today the corrugated iron hanging down so low would have been labelled a health and safety hazard, but in those days no one thought about such things. I was four years old at the time, and not long after he built the shed, I was playing alongside it and gashed my forehead on the sharp edge of the iron roof. An interestingly colourful fountain of blood escaped from my head before I could staunch it with a grubby handkerchief. It hurt, too, and I screamed through my tears. Mum took one look at what I'd done, washed it in cold water, wrapped a bandage round my head and half carried me a mile across town to the hospital. It took several stitches before the doctors were satisfied that I'd be OK. Mum took to calling me her 'wounded soldier', and this made feel a little better – the bandage I wore for a week or two did look impressively soldierly.

The next weekend Dad dismantled the shed and made several trips to the dump with everything piled onto a small cart that he attached to his bike. I still have the scar to this day, along with a second one that I obtained a year or so later through falling over on the seafront on one of our Sunday walks. Fortunately on that occasion we were very close to the hospital. I wore another bandage while Mum hoped and prayed there wouldn't be a third occasion. 'Third time lucky' was one of her pet sayings, and I think it must have been.

I didn't take much notice of the News when it was on the radio, but my dad liked to listen to it, so I did become aware that something called 'The Cold War' kept getting a mention. What on earth was a cold war? And if there was a cold war, could there be a warm war? It was puzzling.

Later I discovered that it wasn't a war as such, but two sides, the East and the West – led by Russia and America respectively – threatening war against each other with a lot of hostile words.

Since the end of World War Two, the world had become an even more dangerous place. Russia and America had developed nuclear bombs, weapons that were capable of destroying all life on planet Earth. Both countries were worried about the other using their weapons first, so to convince the other that it would be a bad idea, each began building more and more. Fortunately this was generally a game of bluff and double bluff, with both sides knowing that if they launched nuclear bombs, the other side would launch them back. In such a situation there would be no winners, and the knowledge of that seemed to keep them in check. However, Russia and America kept their 'fingers on the button', and everyone knew that if a nuclear strike were ordered, there would be a four minute warning before the world was blown to oblivion. Many people began to wonder what they would do if the situation arose and there were only four minutes left to live. For us children, the answer was obvious: eat as many sweets as possible or run wild in a toy shop. Looking back, I suppose this would only have worked if you happened to have a stockpile of sweets near you at the time or were standing outside a toy shop. As children though, we didn't think about the finer details!

I remember one Monday morning in primary school when Caroline, the girl I was sitting next to in class, turned to me, cupped her hands and whispered in my ear, '*Psst*! The world will end on Saturday 11.30pm. Pass it on.'

I was astonished. How did Caroline come to know such an important piece of information? How accurate was it? All day there was a buzz about it in school, and by the end of the day we were convinced that we were living our final week. It was worrying – well, actually it was terrifying. On my return home from school I shared the information with my parents, who looked at each other then told me it certainly wasn't true. They didn't seem worried at all.

At school the next day it didn't seem as if many children had been reassured by anything their parents had said. We were still worried. There didn't seem any reason now for learning spellings or getting maths right, or needing to look smart or be good. What was the point? It would all be over at the weekend. It wouldn't matter if Tottenham won or lost or kept their place in the league. And what would it be like, the end of the world? Would it start with a rumble and crash, would the earth shiver and the ground crack jagged? Would a furnace heat beneath our feet?

These thoughts troubled us all week, and when we finished school for the weekend on Friday afternoon, we were pretty certain that we wouldn't be back on Monday. We said goodbye to each other in the knowledge that it might be for the last time.

Then Saturday came and the weather was warm. The sun blazed and the air shimmered, till the evening sun died red in the west. I tried all sorts of tricks to delay my bedtime. If the world was about to end, then I wanted to be awake, I wanted to be there with Dad and Mum and Chum, not lying in my bed. Mum and Dad went to bed about half past ten, and I was still awake. My mum sat by my bed and eventually I drifted off to sleep.

Sunday morning was truly 'Yabba-dabba do' time. I was Fred Flintstone running around the house, making as much noise as I could. The world hadn't ended, my world hadn't ended. It was such a relief. After breakfast I called on Paul and we sat on the front wall of my garden and marvelled at our survival.

But in the autumn of 1962 such a dangerous situation arose that it seemed like this time there would be no such escape. The world would be plunged into nuclear war. America had discovered that Russian missile launching sites were being built on the island of Cuba just ninety miles from the coast of America. The Cuban leader, Fidel

Castro, was friendly with the Russians and had allowed them to build on his territory. The American President at the time, John F. Kennedy, sent warnings to the Russian leader, Khrushchev, that America would not sit quietly and let this happen. America then set up a naval blockade, or 'quarantine' area, around Cuba to prevent the sites being completed. Russian ships carrying parts for the sites were turned back by the American navy. This brought the two superpowers to the brink of nuclear war as they exchanged threats and counter threats while the world held its breath and waited.

This became known as the Cuban Missile Crisis. I was twelve at the time and discovered a new word: 'Armageddon'. It appeared on the front pages of newspapers whose journalists seemed to be convinced that the end of the world was nigh. I questioned my parents, asking them if we were all about to die, but my father spoke only of the last war, which he had survived. I couldn't take reassurance from that – even I knew that a lot had happened since then. Bombs were bigger, far more destructive and capable of destroying our planet.

My parents were scared too, I could tell. I caught them talking when I came into a room, then stopping very quickly when they saw me. My dad gave my mum an extra cuddle every now and then, but I could see the fear in their eyes. We tiptoed about the house, turned the TV on only to watch the latest news. It didn't seem right somehow to play my records. We needed a good luck charm, and although Elvis Presley sang about one, I doubted this would be enough.

My father said it was prayer that was needed, and so one Sunday evening when the world seemed certain that nuclear war was inevitable, we all went to church. Even though I wasn't sure anymore what I believed in, I prayed with everyone else, prayed so hard it hurt.

When we got home and switched on the TV, the Newsreader told us that President Kennedy had held his nerve and the Russians had backed away. There wouldn't be a war. The world had been saved.

We had a family hug, my dad, my mum and I, while the dog jumped up and barked at us, not understanding what all the fuss was about. We laughed for the first time in days, and relief seemed to flood over me like a warm wave. Later I walked out into the garden, looked up at the sky and whispered a thank you. I stood beneath the stars, breathed in, breathed deep, breathed a future.

CHAPTER EIGHTEEN

How Could Girls Enjoy Being Girls?

As a young boy I used to worry about the fact that half the children at school were girls. Worse, this pattern continued: half the people on our planet were female. How could girls enjoy being girls? They didn't play football, they knew nothing about cars or army or cricket. Their lives seemed to be incredibly dull compared to the fun and adventures that boys had. I decided quite early in life that I really wanted very little to do with them.

Unfortunately I often had to sit next to one in class. This was something that had to be endured, but it was nothing compared to Country Dancing, that dreadful time of the school week when I actually had to hold hands with girls.

I didn't think there was such a thing as a girl worth dancing with. But if we had to choose, there were, even then girls who no one wanted to pair up with, and boys would manoeuvre themselves into places where they might be avoided. No one ever wanted to dance with Gillian, who would burst into tears at the slightest thing. Our teacher would always blame the boy who partnered her, and – most times – it wasn't his fault. Boys in the 1950s weren't made for dancing. We had two left feet which kicked ankles and trod on sensitive toes. It was pure hell, and I was always glad when the lesson was over and there were seven days before it came round again.

We had two playgrounds in our school, and a stretch of no man's land separated the boys' playground from the one containing these strangely behaved creatures called girls. From what we could see, girls had a really boring time of it, with their hula-hoops, walking on hands or skipping to the chant of some silly rhyme.

At playtime there would always be a teacher patrolling the place where the playgrounds joined. In winter she'd be cradling coffee and stamping to keep out the cold. If she were called away to check a fight, tend a nosebleed or give medical help to someone whose handstand had gone horribly wrong, there would be open war along the line.

We threw things from playground to playground: halves of sandwiches, snowballs or paper planes with the words 'Ronnie loves Rosemary' written on each wing. He didn't, of course, but we pinned him down while we wrote it.

If Mr Mankelow saw us, he'd tell us to 'Stop acting the goat'. It was his favourite phrase, and we'd run round the playground, fingers on heads like horns, pretending to butt each other.

Each morning us boys had to cross the girls' playground to reach our own, and every time it was push or be pushed, shove or be shoved. Worse still was if you were captured by a gang of girls intent on getting you to join in their game of kiss chase. There was one girl in particular who nobody wanted to be kissed by. Horror of horrors if you suffered a sloppy kiss from her. You'd look in the mirror and finger the spot for weeks, hoping it wouldn't grow warty or worse. I wasn't too sure what this girl had done to deserve being singled out in this way, but she was, and I sort of felt a little sorry for her. Once, one boy was dragged kicking and screaming to the girls' toilets. 'What was it like?' we asked him when they finally let him go. He seemed unable to answer. It must have been awful.

Paul and I got into trouble once for chasing a girl

called Josephine. She was rather annoying in the classroom, always putting her hand up and showing off, always telling tales in a whiny sort of voice. She seemed to think she knew everything, and the smirk on her face when she was proved right irritated all of us. She went home the same way as us, and in the past we'd completely ignored her. But on this occasion it seemed like a good idea to chase after her, zoom past on either side and grab the hat that she was wearing. Once we had hold of her hat, we weren't sure what to do with it, so we frisbeed it to each other for a bit while she played piggy in the middle, trying unsuccessfully to retrieve it. After a while she gave up, and we could see that she was crying. Paul tried to give back her hat, but she wouldn't take it from him. Instead she started running away from us. We looked at each other, looked at the hat, and then chased after her.

When we reached the street where she lived, we hung back. We certainly didn't want to get a tongue lashing from her mum or dad.

We watched from behind a parked car as her front door opened and Josephine stumbled inside. Her mother peered out but failed to spot us, and then closed the door. I looked at Paul. We still had Josephine's hat. We crept forward and gently hung the hat on the door knocker. Then we let the knocker fall and raced back to our hiding place.

Nothing happened at first, and we were just about to move off when the door opened and Josephine's mum reappeared, pulling Josephine behind her.

They took down the hat, looked around and then walked off down the street. When they turned the corner we came out of hiding and followed. From the corner we glimpsed them crossing the road and carrying on in the same direction as we needed to go to reach our homes.

We trailed them, keeping a good distance, till they turned into the street where we lived. We looked at each other. It was obvious now: Josephine's mother was about to complain about us. But how did she know where we lived? Just at that moment my next door neighbour appeared in his garden. Josephine's mother said something to him, and he pointed towards my house. The next thing we knew, they were through the garden and ringing my door bell.

We crept closer and hid behind a van parked outside my neighbour's house. It was just possible to hear Josephine's mother's raised voice. According to her, we were picking on her daughter. We felt rather annoyed by this complaint, as today had been the first time we'd chased her. We couldn't hear what my mother was saying, but whatever it was, it didn't seem to be the right thing as Josephine's mother's voice got louder and louder. Finally she stormed back down the garden path with Josephine behind her, and we edged round the van to make sure they didn't spot us.

I wasn't too keen on going indoors because I was sure I'd get a telling off from my mum, and in the end Paul came with me. My mum didn't say anything, just acted as if there was nothing wrong. We ate some cake that she'd made and watched TV. When Paul left she said, 'Best not to chase that girl again, Brian. I know it was just fun for you two, but her mother seems to think otherwise.' I readily agreed, relieved that I'd got off so lightly.

Later, when Dad came home, I heard her telling him about the visit. I also heard the words 'silly woman' and 'kids will be kids'.

Paul and I tried to ignore Josephine after that, but a month or so later, she told tales on a friend of ours, and we decided that we would chase her again. This we did, until suddenly Josephine turned and faced us. 'Come on then,' she said. 'Who's going to give me a kiss?' Paul and I looked at each other and then back at the pair of lips puckered in expectation. This really was an unexpected turn of events, and certainly an invitation which we were both reluctant to accept. She opened her arms and moved towards us. We backed away, slowly at first but then faster, hearing the sound of laughter behind us. Obviously her mother had suggested a new strategy. It was Josephine's secret weapon and her moment of triumph.

A year or two later, when my views about girls were beginning to change slightly, I started noticing Sally. She lived a few doors away from me and had long blonde hair that she seemed to hide behind so that it was hard to catch a glimpse of her face. She was probably a year or so older than me and considered me a kid, but that didn't stop me from imagining her as my girlfriend.

Some days I'd be walking along the street and I'd see Sally heading towards me. In my room at night I'd rehearse all kinds of witty opening lines, thinking I might be able to say something brilliant that would make her notice me, something funny that would make her smile, but I didn't dare try. Words formed in my mouth but grew to the size of boulders, and I just couldn't slide them past my tongue. I knew if I tried to speak I would falter, stutter and make a 'pig's ear' of it (another of my mum's sayings, which she used a lot when things went wrong – where it comes from, I've no idea!). I would turn red with embarrassment and quickly move off. I'd then spend all evening working out why I made such a mess of things and how I should have done better. It was no good – the twelve year old me was useless around girls.

So I contented myself with watching Sally from my bedroom window. Beneath the window was the desk where I did my homework. I'd shifted it there so I could spot the slightest sign of movement from Sally's house while I worked. I could see the path that led from her door to the garden gate, and though often it would be her mum or her dad or her little sister on the path, occasionally, joy of joys, it was Sally herself. She was a vision I could hardly take my eyes off, even though I still hadn't really seen the face behind the hair. In my dreams I'd be with her, making her smile, making her laugh, and I knew she'd be gorgeous.

These days I'd probably be labelled something nasty because of all the time I spent watching Sally, but I had nothing but warm feelings for her, and a glimpse of her face, well, her hair left me with a wistful longing that one day she might see me for the brilliant, talented and handsome lad that I undoubtedly was.

However, the real problem was, I knew, that I *wasn't* attractive to girls. I was the original ugly duckling hiding in the reeds and waiting for the day that he might turn into a swan. I was gawky and my ears were large, like jug handles. My hair stood up in places where it shouldn't and refused to stay down even with dollops of hair cream. When I walked, I shuffled and looked down at the ground. It was useless, I knew. Sally was unobtainable, out of my league, but she brightened my days and I was grateful for that.

Later on, when I was sixteen and still keen on her, I wrote Sally a poem. In fact, the first poem I ever wrote was for her. I spent hours and hours composing it until one day, when I knew I'd never do any better, I decided to deliver it. I copied it out neatly, folded it and stuck it in an envelope. When it got dark, I sneaked up the road and pushed it through her letterbox. I waited one day, two days, a week... but she couldn't have been impressed. Later, I found out why, when I saw her walking out with someone else, someone I knew. He was two years older than me and had his own motorbike. I knew no good would ever come of it. I worried for Sally, that she'd made the wrong choice, went for 'flash' instead of 'steady'. I soon got over it, but for a week or so it did hurt, that first rejection. Fortunately it didn't stop me writing more poems!

CHAPTER NINETEEN

I'm A Crud, Sir

The grammar school that I attended was a tall red brick building in the centre of Ramsgate. It had extensive school grounds and fortunately was only a five minute walk from where I lived. It had been used as a hospital for Canadian troops during World War One and was surrounded by spiky black railings. There was a rumour that someone had once jumped from the top floor of the building and impaled himself on the spikes below, but I never found out whether there was any truth in this.

When our wheezing, arthritic headmaster decided that a boy deserved a beating there was a certain master who was always called upon. Rumour had it that he would carefully pace out a run up, rather like a fast bowler does on the cricket field, before turning and hurtling back at lightning speed to deliver a fearsome blow to the unfortunate backside.

I counted myself lucky to have never experienced his technique.

Other masters had their own ways of maintaining discipline. Our maths teacher, Mr Jones, threw chalk. Over the years he had become incredibly skilful at placing a piece of chalk exactly where he wanted it, and I saw him, on various occasions, ping chalk onto the desk of a boy so that it bounced back up and hit him on the nose. It was rumoured that several years before one boy had needed hospital treatment to remove a piece of chalk that had become lodged in his nostril.

On other occasions Jonesy, as we called him, would lob the board rubber at some unfortunate who wasn't paying attention. Again, he had perfected this so that the board rubber would land on the boy's desk, resulting in an explosion of chalk dust that quickly settled on the unfortunate boy's jacket, face and in his hair. Then, if that wasn't considered punishment enough, the boy would be asked to return the board rubber to Jonesy's outstretched hand. All eyes watched as Jonesy then dropped the rubber on the floor. 'Pick it up,' he'd snarl. Then, as the boy bent to pick it up, Jonesy, depending on how he felt, would either a) Push the boy's backside with his foot so that he toppled over onto the floor, or b) Whack him with the flat of the blackboard compass.

Our chemistry teacher, Mr Williams, called everybody 'crud'. 'What are you boy?' he'd ask if you gave him a dumb answer or failed to do something properly in the lab. 'I'm a crud, sir,' you would need to answer back and, for some strange reason I never worked out, that kept him happy. (According to *Cassell's Dictionary of Slang*, the word 'crud' means 'anything or anyone worthless' – so that's what he thought of us!)

He also referred to any piece of equipment in the laboratory as 'gubbins.' 'You boy,' he'd call, 'bring me the gubbins.' Problem was that often we didn't know which piece of equipment he was asking us to bring him, and then we'd have to admit again to being a 'crud' before he pointed out what he wanted.

Classes with Mr Williams never seemed to have disciplinary problems, but he always seemed to be inventing fresh tortures in the laboratory. One, which I remember vividly, and which gave me nightmares, was to measure out a quantity of sulphuric acid using a glass tube called a 'pipette'.

Mr Williams had already told us about sulphuric acid.

'Spill it on your hands,' he'd said, 'And it will burn them.' There was a story I'd heard from another school in the town where a boy had had his pen filled up with sulphuric acid. He'd been rushed to hospital when it leaked all over his fingers. So what on earth was our teacher doing asking us to suck up the stuff into a tube? I'd be bound to do it wrong and get a mouthful. This was unbelievable. I just couldn't begin to think what it would do to the inside of my mouth.

The night before we were timetabled to submit ourselves to this torture, my mother could see that something was worrying me. After some token resistance, I told her what it was. 'I've never heard anything more ridiculous,' she said. 'There's no way you're doing that.' In the end, we agreed that I should miss school the next day. I was so relieved.

As it happened, there were several boys whose parents must have thought the same as mine, but those who braved the ordeal seemed to survive OK.

All this would be unthinkable behaviour from teachers today, but back then, when I was a teenager, nobody questioned it.

Another of my teachers was a Mr Parker. Honestly, wouldn't you think that you would change a name like that before you went into teaching? Inevitably we nicknamed him 'Nosey', and cries of 'Watch out, Nosey's coming' were regularly heard in the corridors. Mr

Parker's problem was that he was a really pleasant man. He hated violence of any kind and simply wanted to be our friend. We, of course, were far too young to appreciate this kind gesture. We made his life hell on many occasions, and looking back, I really regret it.

Our history teacher was Mr Michaels, who wore a black gown whenever he taught us. He was ancient and looked as if he'd stepped down from the dog-eared history books that he kept up on high shelves. Those of us who had seen pictures of the Victorian Prime Minister Lord Palmerston knew for sure that he must have been a descendent. You could tell from the way he strode along the corridor and in the way he commanded the room from his place on a raised platform where his desk sat. Anyone silly enough to do something wrong would find themselves hypnotised by his gaze. He wouldn't say anything, but you knew that whatever crime had been committed would not be repeated.

In his gown, his dark suit, his Victorian 'tash' and with his 'Manners maketh man' lectures, Mr Michaels unlocked the secrets of history, breathing life into the dull and the dreary, making it seem like we were there. We felt that we were looking over the shoulders of monarchs and presidents as they signed their documents and issued their decrees, or waiting in tents the night before the Battle of Waterloo. We were thigh high in mud in Flanders Fields or baying for blood at the steps of the guillotine. It didn't hurt that he looked like he belonged in many of the scenes he described! But he was a wonderful teacher, and talking to him one to one, I knew, as he did, that I would be hooked on the subject for life, that I would love history just as he did. I have plenty to thank him for.

I only saw a boy get the better of him on one occasion, when there was an advertising campaign going on for Esso petrol. The ads tried to convince everyone that their fuel had the power of a tiger. So it was wonderful, one day, to see Mr Michaels in his school gown, striding down the corridor towards the staffroom with a sticker on his back that announced: 'I've got a tiger in my tank'.

Our music teacher, Mr Samuels, was passionate about his subject, but he was on a road to nowhere with us. He was bald, so inevitably we called him 'Baldy'. He was passionate about his subject, but unlike Mr Michaels, he just didn't have the skill to put his enthusiasm across to teenage boys. We'd troop into his room and sit down, arms folded, absolutely determined not to show a flicker of interest in what he had to offer us. Occasionally he'd ask us what sort of music we liked. 'BEATLES!' we'd yell out, 'STONES, KINKS, ANIMALS...' 'They're all savages,' he'd reply. That was his favourite word to describe rock groups. ' Won't last.' he'd say, 'Ten years time they'll all be forgotten.' I was familiar with this line of argument. My dad used to say the same every time *Top of the Pops* came on the TV.

So week by week, we put up with Mr Samuels, and he put up with us as he tried and failed to interest us in Brahms or Handel or Beethoven. 'The melody's OK,' I remember one boy saying about a piece by Mozart, 'but I wish he'd written some lyrics.' No doubt Mr Samuels was anticipating the day that he could retire and leave us little heathens behind. He often slipped into a sort of trance when he was playing music for us, probably dreaming of any place other than where he was – a concert hall, a tropical isle, a shady forest. The music transported him, far away from the school room.

We, of course, took full advantage of this. Paper planes would be taken from pockets and school bags and the room would be filled with flying missiles. Several boys would add weight to the nose cones of their planes so that they would cause the maximum discomfort if they collided with someone's face. Most times Mr Samuels seemed to sleep though it all, but on one occasion, a plane veered off course and hit him right on the nose. No one, of course, owned up, and even though we suspected who had done it, no one was prepared to say. 'Right,' he said, 'I want the whole class in detention, Friday after school.' It didn't seem quite so funny then.

Then there was Mr Rankin, another Maths teacher. Mr Rankin was a spitter. The letter 'S' was a particular problem for him. We knew that if we were going to do work on symmetry or subtraction, or any other area of maths that included a lot of 'S' words, then the front row would be in for a soaking. Nobody wanted to be late for Mr Rankin's lessons. The room would fill up from the back, and anyone arriving late would have to sit in the danger zone. A whole year was spent trying to avoid the front seats in Mr Rankin's lessons. I remember one particular occasion when five boys turned up for his lesson wearing plastic macs and rain hats. They deliberately placed themselves in the front row and one even opened up an umbrella. Looking back now, of course, I cringe at how cruel this was, but to teenage boys it was hilarious. We expected Mr Rankin to blow his top, we hoped for a volcanic reaction, but there was nothing like that. Very quietly he slid into his seat at the master's desk. His shoulders slumped and he looked both sad and confused. Then he stood up again, reached for some chalk and wrote everyone's names on the board. Next to them he wrote, 'Detention Friday'. Then he left the room.

Moments later our headteacher walked in and told us how disappointed he was in all of us. Not just the mac wearers, but the rest of us too, because we had done nothing to stop them.

The next day Mr Rankin was back with us again, and nothing else was said. But I felt sorry for him and hoped that I could make amends somehow. I never did, and we soon found other ways to annoy him, as boys always do.

By far the worst teacher of all was an ex-regimental

sergeant major, Mr Jackson. He took us for PE. I'll never forget my first lesson with him. It seemed as if us new boys had arrived at our secondary school to be greeted by a demon from hell! 'There will be no slackers in my PE lessons,' he told us right from the start. 'Everyone does everything, no excuses. And don't start bringing me any notes from your mumsy-wumsies telling me that you've got a bit of a chill or you've hurt your little toe, because do you know what I do with them? I tear them up!'

We looked at each other and shivered.

Then out came the vaulting horse. 'Right,' said Mr Jackson (for reasons that will become obvious, he came to be known as 'Mad Jack'). 'I want everyone getting over this by the end of the lesson or you'll meet my friend.' Mad Jack's friend was a baseball bat, and it looked about as friendly as a street gang on a Saturday night. One by one we ran at the horse, jumped onto a springboard, leapt the horse and landed gracefully on a mat. Or we tried to, anyway. About a quarter of the class managed it while the rest of us collided with the horse, slipped off it sideways or generally mistimed our leaps. One boy who, as Mad Jack put it, was carrying 'a sack of potatoes around his middle' opened his legs and landed on the horse so heavily that he had to be taken away to matron, where he spent the next hour with an ice pack pressed tightly against his tender parts.

Mad Jack allowed us all one chance, and then if we made a mess of it, he would 'help' us. 'Help' consisted of swinging his baseball bat against our bottoms in the firm belief that the shock would propel us over the horse.

It was terrifying and I never got the hang of it. Once over the horse we were supposed to climb a rope and touch the gym ceiling before sliding back down and lining up at the horse once more. Climbing a rope wasn't too difficult for me, but you had to be careful coming back down. You had to do it slowly. If you didn't your hands felt as if they were on fire. One or two boys discovered this the hard way, and their reactions were enough for us to learn our lesson too.

Being able to climb a rope was my salvation. I found that I was capable of hanging around at the top for as long as I wanted. My hands and feet gripped the rope tightly, and whilst I was up there, I was out of the line of Mad Jack's vision. I could miss a few turns at the horse without him realizing.

For any boy who was fit and could do what was required, then Mad Jack was no threat, but for those of us who were weedy or nerdy or who carried too much weight, he made PE lessons hell. Fortunately, in years eight and nine of secondary school, we were spared Mad Jack's treatment. Another PE teacher took us, Mr Hardy, and he was brilliant. He was kind, compassionate, always concerned that we shouldn't overstretch ourselves, and most of all, when we did achieve something we thought we couldn't do, he was as excited as we were.

Later on, in my first year of sixth form, we were timetabled to have Mad Jack for our one lesson of PE each week. I didn't turn up for the first lesson, I forget why, but by some stroke of good fortune, he hadn't got a register of who should be with him, so he simply wrote down the names of everybody there and then used that. I quickly realized that if my name wasn't on the register then I was an 'invisible man' and there was no need for me to attend. So I truanted his lessons for the whole year, and he was none the wiser! I have my classmates to thank too, because nobody ratted on me. They were probably wishing they could do the same thing!

On the last day of our time at secondary school, we finally got our own back on Mad Jack for all the hurt, discomfort, worry and sleepless nights his bully boy tactics had given us. We were walking through the staff car park, out of sight of the school building, when we noticed his Mini. Next to it was a raised concrete platform about forty centimetres above the ground, where one of the entrances to the tunnel system had been covered over. We looked at the platform then at Jack's car. Would it be possible to lift his car onto the platform and leave it there for him to find?

It took ten of us, but we did it! We walked away whistling, knowing that our parting gift to Jack would give him a real headache. We wondered if he'd figure out how his car got there, and better still, whether he'd be able to work out how on earth he was going to get it off again!

And finally, there was a jewel among masters: Ken Girkin, my geography teacher in the sixth form. He was a teacher you respected one hundred percent because it was quite clear that he respected you. He gave up a huge amount of his time to make sure you understood precisely anything that had proved difficult. Lunchtime or after school, he was always ready to put in extra hours to make sure that you were confident about what you were doing. From the moment we entered his class, we knew that this was a different type of teacher. 'Call me Ken,' he offered, and Ken he was for the next two years. I'm not quite sure what the other teachers thought about this, but it didn't seem to worry Ken – he just went his own sweet way. I have a lot to thank him for. I was pretty shy in those days, but he helped raise my confidence.

We had a school song that was meant to make us feel proud and uplifted. It was sung at the ends of terms or on special occasions. The masters would be seated on stage, and I suppose the idea was that the rousing lift of their voices would inspire the boys. But it never really happened that way! In fact, some of the masters seemed to 'sing' as if their mouths were taped up tight or full of stodgy dough. One or two voices were in evidence – the head in particular always raised his voice to the rafters – but we got the impression that many of the staff were even less enthusiastic about the school song than we were.

The first lines of the song were:

Here where the feet of Englishmen first trod the English soil
And marched in strong battalions on the foe...

Some boys, more creative than myself at the time, composed alternative versions of the song, which although not quite so stirring, were nevertheless sung in a more lively manner. You could see the Head bristling as he detected far less respectful versions welling up from different parts of the hall.

Daft really, but it amused us greatly at the time.

— CHAPTER TWENTY —

Billy

I could have walked right past him. I could have walked past him a hundred times or more without a flicker of recognition.

I could have heard his voice across a crowded room or on a busy train and been none the wiser. I could have been served by him in a shop and still wouldn't have made the connection. And yet he's been with me all these years, like a shadow walking beside me. Not a constant shadow, rather one that comes and goes, one that's keeping pace for a while and then out of step.

Until I left Primary School I didn't realise how happy I'd been there. True, there had been upsets, troubles, worries, but nothing to compare to my first three years at secondary school. When I wasn't trying to dodge Mad Jack's baseball bat, I was dodging Billy. Billy the bully. Billy who made life miserable for dozens of kids at secondary school. Billy who always seemed to be there, despite what you did to avoid him. Billy who ruled the bogs. Billy, King of the toilets. To this day I can't think what it was that made the toilets so attractive to Billy. They stank for a start, but he didn't seem to notice. He was in there at break times; he was in there at lesson times. He was like a hideous spider just waiting to pull you into his web. I knew boys who wet themselves just to avoid risking what Billy had to offer.

Billy was a gorilla in a school uniform, a uniform that was always too short in the sleeves and too tight around the chest. His trousers were always stained with mud and grass, and his shirt was always missing buttons. Occasionally he left the toilets and lumbered into some poor teacher's lesson, where he caused havoc by flicking ears or shooting chewed up balls of paper through a home-made blowpipe. I think this was why the teachers let Billy spend so much time in the toilets – an absent Billy was far preferable to having him in class.

I once walked past his house with my dad, and we both discovered a bigger version of Billy knocking his son around the garden. I guess that this was why Billy felt this was the right way to behave. He got bullied himself, so he'd pass on that treatment to others. And he did pass it on, whenever and wherever he could.

Billy and his family lived on Paradise Street. I ask you, who in their right mind would call somewhere Paradise Street? I can imagine Paradise Street as the name of a street running alongside the ocean in Los Angeles, or in Hawaii – somewhere with sunshine and views of sand and surf. But Ramsgate, alongside the cold English Channel, where the wind blew straight from the Arctic at times, was certainly not a fitting place! Paradise was not a word that could be linked to any road in Ramsgate as far as I was concerned. The road I grew up in certainly wouldn't have suited it, and Paradise Street itself looked shabby, uninviting, and with Billy living there, about as far from paradise as it was possible to get. As I wrote in a poem recently:

Paradise Street in our town
was a street you didn't go down.

All the boys I was warned not to play with
lived on Paradise Street.

All the boys who swore,
who wore scars like fashion accessories,
who didn't need a reason to beat you up

or knock you down,
they all lived on Paradise Street.

Paradise Street was a short cut from one part of town to another, but I didn't use it. To my mind, anyone going down there alone could be walking into a trap. No one wanted to find out what would happen if you got caught by Billy. So we all kept clear of Paradise Street, and kept on keeping clear of it.

There were, I discovered, three ways of dealing with Billy. Three ways of coping with Billy in your life. The first was to run and keep on running, fast as you could. Billy wasn't fit. He found it hard to break into a sprint and was easily winded. I could run fast in those days, and I did. I took to running around town, past dark alleyways where he might be lurking. I ran to school and ran home again at night. I must have been fit!

But Billy, although he didn't look it, was clever in different ways. He'd work out regular routes and times, and position himself where you would least expect to find him. You'd be haring it down one street, turn a corner, then BAM – you'd realise that all your speed was actually taking you right to him.

The second way of dealing with Billy was to turn and fight him. I longed to be able to learn some unusual fighting technique that would allow me to deliver a crushing blow, the kind that Billy would never forget, the kind that he certainly wouldn't want to receive again. But I was too much of a wimp to ever do more than dream.

I read about heroes in comics. Comics were full of heroes who threw themselves into the heat of battle and emerged without a scratch. There was one guy who always wielded a cricket bat and would knock all around him for six. I wished I knew where to contact him. I would have happily employed him to sort out Billy and his gang. I cut out his pictures from the comics and wove new stories around them. Stories where Billy was punched, flattened, knocked down, tied to railway tracks and tortured in every hideous way that I could think of. I fell asleep at night with these images in my head.

Once a girl he'd annoyed kicked Billy right in the place where it really hurts. I didn't see this happen, but those who did told how Billy howled like a dog, rolled himself up into a ball and shed real tears. But there were some things that boys just didn't do to each other, even to bullies. And of course, though Billy never went near the girl again, he made life hell for her younger brother.

Those who did turn and fight Billy always came off worst. You'd always know when a boy had had enough. They'd appear the next day with black eyes or bloodied noses. And that was just the start. They were marked men from then on. Billy showed no respect for anyone who fought him, just a grim determination to show them who was boss once again as soon as possible.

The third way of dealing with Billy was to join his gang. For some boys this was the only possible option, the only way that they had of surviving the daily ordeal. But Billy wouldn't take anyone into his gang. You had to prove yourself first, and Billy's warped brain was forever thinking up new tests for wannabe gang members. Maybe you'd have to steal something from a shop, perhaps coin a master's car (run a coin along the paintwork to leave a lengthy scratch). Doing Billy's dirty work meant that you gained Billy's protection. He'd leave you alone so long as you kept on doing what he asked.

As a member of the gang you'd be involved in Billy's initiation ceremonies for new year sevens. Everyone heard about Billy and what he had in store for you before they arrived at secondary school. But if you talked to your mum about it, she would tell you not to be so daft. Of course he doesn't do that, he wouldn't be allowed to. But teachers had no control over Billy and turned a blind eye.

The first day at this new school was terrifying enough without Billy. There were over two hundred of us crammed into the school hall in our shiny new uniforms, our caps and blazers, our first pairs of long trousers. We were carrying our school bags with the equipment we'd been asked to buy – rulers, pens, pencils – all rattling around inside. There was little noise as we'd no idea whether it was permitted to make any.

On the stage in front of us the masters assembled in

their black gowns, waiting for their classes to be called out. I was hoping that I'd be in a class with Richard, who I'd known since starting primary school. But this was not to be. Names were called out and one by one my friends left with their new classes. I was in the last class to be called, and once in the classroom I found myself sitting next to a boy who said his name was Greg.

At break time I wandered out to the yard with Greg. He too had heard about Billy, and both of us kept well away from the toilets.

But Richard didn't, and Billy was there waiting for him, along with the other members of his gang. Five minutes later, when he reappeared, Richard was soaking wet and sobbing uncontrollably.

Later he told us what had happened. He'd been caught by three of Billy's gang – Johnny Angel – a baby faced boy who nevertheless had superhuman strength, Fingers Fletcher – so called because when his fingers got to work on you, the bruises were there for weeks – and Gerry the Ghoul, who really did look like an extra for a late night horror movie. If the three of them grabbed you, there was nothing you could do. You stayed grabbed; there was no chance of escape.

Richard was small for his age, and I imagined Johnny picking him up, tucking him under his arm and walking with him, flanked by Fingers and Gerry. He was taken, to the toilets, of course, to be set in front of Billy, who told him of his crime – the crime of being a new boy – and then outlined what his punishment was to be.

It must have been incredibly crowded in the cubicle that they led him to, but somehow they managed to lift Richard off his feet and then dunk him head first into the toilet bowl, like a living loo brush. We listened in horror as he told how he'd started to scream and then quickly clamped his mouth shut in case any of the ghastly water slipped between his teeth. Three times he was immersed, and on the final dunking Billy flushed the chain.

We all looked at each other. Nobody spoke. I knew that everybody was thinking the same thing as me. How on earth could we avoid what Richard had gone through? It was really the stuff of nightmares. What were the teachers doing about it? Didn't they care?

I was luckier than many boys because I was able to go home for lunch, where I could make use of our toilet. I just didn't know how boys managed to go the whole day without peeing. My house was only a five minute walk from the school, and in the hour we had at lunchtime, I could comfortably walk home, eat my lunch, and then return to school for ten minutes of footy.

One morning, however, I just couldn't contain myself any longer. I must have drunk too much at breakfast time, and I was almost doubled up in agony. I'd have to go or run the real risk of wetting myself. I'd seen that happen before in primary school to a girl who never recovered from the embarrassment. I had to put my hand up and ask to be excused. I was terrified. Billy wasn't in class that day, which meant that he was either playing truant or he was hiding out in the boys' toilets. If he was hiding, then I would be walking straight into a trap. And if his gang were there too... The prospect of being dunked head first into an evil-smelling toilet was just too horrific. But what could I do?

I found the answer to my problem as I hurried along the corridor. In front of me was the door to the masters' toilet. Without giving it any further thought I pushed the door open and scooted inside. I hadn't thought at all what I'd do or say if I found someone in the toilet, but fortunately it was empty. I raced for a cubicle and quickly locked the door. If someone comes in now, I thought, I'll be trapped. But it was the middle of a lesson, so most teachers would be in their classrooms, I reasoned.

Oh, what relief. I did what I had to do, safe from Billy and his gang, but just as I was about to flush the chain, I heard the outer door open and someone walk in. I held my breath. Where was he heading?

Footsteps moved towards me and whoever it was came into the cubicle next to mine. I froze. Did he know there was someone else in here? I waited until I heard the sort of sounds that convinced me that the mystery figure was doing what he needed to do. Then, without daring to flush the chain, I eased open the lock on the door and dashed out. No way could I wash my hands. My mum would have been very disapproving. *Sorry Mum*, I thought, *but it's a life or death situation.*

I pulled open the door and was about to make my escape when I realised that there was somebody heading down the corridor towards me. I shut the door quickly and waited on the inside, looking and listening for signs that whoever was in the cubicle would be emerging soon. It was a situation I'd read about in books, where someone would write, 'He was trapped between the devil and the deep blue sea.' That was me all right.

I heard the chain flush behind me, and I looked around desperately for somewhere to hide. There was another door! I pulled the handle and it opened. I dived inside, pulling the door shut behind me. I was in some sort of cupboard, but as I moved to make myself more comfortable, I dislodged something heavy that fell on me. I overbalanced against the door, which swung open, and I tumbled out of the cupboard and onto the floor, accompanied by an avalanche of toilet rolls that rained down on top of me.

As I scrabbled around, trying to gain control of as many toilet rolls as I could, I became aware that a tall figure was leaning over me.

'Hold still,' he said. 'I'll help you.'

Oh miracles of miracles, it was Mr Hardy, our kind, compassionate PE teacher.

'What on earth were you doing in there?' he asked, his eyes twinkling with amusement. 'No, don't tell me, let me guess. Were you counting toilet rolls for a maths project? Were you testing the darkness as part of a science lesson? Or were you finding out what it must have been like to have been locked away in a prison cell?'

I looked at the floor and said nothing. 'Now you must have had a reason,' he said. 'I won't be angry if you tell me the truth.'

So I told him.

'I suspected that might be happening,' he said. 'I haven't been a teacher for best part of twenty years without being able to work out one or two things. Leave it with me and I'll look into it. Now, where should you be? I'm sure you'll be told off for being away from your lesson for so long, so let me see if I can smooth things over with your teacher.'

And he did.

I wish I could report that things improved after that. But they didn't. Billy was a law unto himself, and even Mr Hardy couldn't control him. Pleased to be rid of him, teachers would still let him slip out of lessons, and no one followed up where he went. And so Billy remained tyrant of the toilets.

Going home after school was a dangerous time too. Billy would be waiting somewhere. He always managed to be out of school and away before the rest of us. He'd be after money most of the time, change from dinner money or from the sweet money that my mother had given me so I could call into the shop and buy sweets on the way home from school.

Leaving school and going home was like a commando excursion into enemy territory. First, we'd sort out who would be walking (or running) home with who. Nobody wanted to risk a lone encounter with Billy and his gang. Then, once this was settled, we'd set off, stopping at every corner to peek round and check for Billy. Any sign that he was around would mean that we'd need to find another way home

Quite often this meant taking a short cut through other people's gardens. This was not without casualties. Someone would tread on a prize marrow or run into some roses. Others would find clothes lines in their way and have to fight clear of the flapping shirts. There would be a commotion from the house as the owners realised that their garden was being invaded, and for a short time we'd forget about Billy and concentrate on escaping elderly gardeners. There would be much fist waving and gesticulating, but we knew they'd never catch us. We were far too fast.

Sometimes we'd cut through the allotments, places where people without much garden could grow their own flowers and vegetables. Here there were hazards like runner bean poles that would suddenly loom up in front of us, and carefully positioned trellises that would collapse on top of us. Or we'd stumble into a chicken run and send its inhabitants fluttering and squawking in all directions.

But generally there was safety in numbers. Occasionally we'd hear stories, how Billy and his gang locked someone up in a garden shed and left him there, how there had been a spitting contest with some small boy as the target, or how Billy had set fire to somebody's bag. These stories, of course, just fuelled Billy's reputation. He was awful. We knew he was awful and little that we heard about him could surprise us.

Then one Monday we came to school and Billy wasn't there. In two years of grammar school, he'd always been there. We couldn't believe it. Someone plucked up courage and asked Johnny Angel, but he didn't know either. The news spread round. 'It's a Billy-free day!' The tension eased, we relaxed a bit, even risked the toilets. It wouldn't last though; he'd be back again tomorrow, like a bad penny. That was another of my mother's favourite sayings. 'It'll turn up again like a bad penny.' I never found out what she meant. How could a penny be good or bad? If I found a penny it was always good news for me.

We were nervous walking to school the next day. We looked for Billy round every corner, reasoning that he'd be making up for lost time, taking more sweets or more money from us than he usually did. But again, he wasn't there. Maybe he'd caught some disease and was lying flat out in hospital. Maybe it would be weeks till he reappeared. A second Billy-freeday – we couldn't believe our luck.

Billy wasn't in school on Wednesday either, or Thursday. When he was absent again on Friday, there was almost a carnival atmosphere around school. Nobody worried about looking over their shoulders to see if Billy was stalking them. We used the toilets as we liked, and although they smelled just as bad, there was no stink of fear. Billy was gone and his mates seemed just as puzzled as we were. Without Billy there to direct them, they seemed lost, unwilling to organise anything themselves. They went to lessons and left us alone.

The following Monday there was again no sign of Billy. We huddled together in the playground imagining all kinds of dire circumstances. Maybe he'd been hit by a car when playing Chicken (last one to cross the road before a car goes past). He seemed to think he was some kind of champion at this. We just thought he was crazy risking his life in such a way. Maybe he'd robbed a bank and was hiding from the police, or been eaten by a crocodile at the zoo, or abducted by aliens.

Halfway through the morning we discovered the real reason. Someone asked Mr Parker, thinking that if anyone knew the answer it would be 'Nosey.'

'He's left our school, gone away for good.'

There was a moment of silence while we took in the news. This was followed by a huge cheer. Billy gone! Gone for good! We just couldn't believe our luck.

Nosey didn't even try to teach us after that. He couldn't quieten us down; we were far too busy talking about what this would mean for us all. Later we learnt that Billy's dad must have switched jobs – the whole family had moved to another town. Billy, of course, had said nothing about the move, although he must have known about it for weeks.

Sometimes we'd find ourselves thinking about Billy: where he might have gone, which school he was attending. No doubt he was making life unpleasant for others, but we didn't let the thought bother us for long. As long as it wasn't us, we really didn't care.

CHAPTER TWENTY-ONE

Pick It Up & Run With It

I wasn't looking forward to games lessons at secondary school – I'd heard too much about them already. I prayed it wouldn't be with Mad Jack, because his first PE lesson had been terrifying.

Fortunately I was in Mr Hardy's group for games, and it was his job to teach us rugby. Why not football? You needed to be tough to play rugby, and I wasn't! I just wasn't built for it. I was the original five-stone weakling,

229

the one who would get sand kicked in his face the moment he sat down on a beach. I wished I had some muscles so I didn't look quite so skinny.

Yet there was one advantage to being skinny: I wouldn't be picked to play in the scrum. In the scrum someone could beat you up and no one would know. No one would hear you yell amidst the grunts and shouts from everyone else. You could be elbowed or throttled. You could have your ears scraped and stretched till they felt as if they were being pulled away from your head. You could have someone's vice-like grip on a part of you that should never be squeezed in such a way. The scrum would break up, leaving you writhing on the ground. And while you were lying there in desperate need of a block of ice to hold against your private parts, the scrum would come charging back the opposite way, leaving you trampled and flattened by huge studded boots. The impression of someone's studs on the fleshy part of your leg would take days to disappear.

Fortunately I could run fast. All that pounding the streets trying to keep clear of Billy must have done me some good. So I was chosen as a winger, and whenever the ball came in my direction, I had to pick it up and run with it as fast as I could. Really though, all I wanted to do was to get rid of it as quickly as I could before some hulking great member of the opposing team's scrum knocked me down and then sat on me.

I never understood rugby and certainly never got to enjoy it, particularly in winter, when the ground was either rock hard after weeks of frost, or churned to thick mud after torrential rain. What made it even worse was that, although we had games pitches in our school grounds, for some mad reason we had to be bussed out to play on pitches on high ground, where the wind would seem to blow from every direction. Ramsgate, being on the east coast of England, suffered howling gales that seemingly blew from the depths of icy Russia.

Even on the coldest of days we would only be allowed to wear shorts and a shirt. This might have been OK if we'd have gone straight out for a run to warm us up, but for some strange reason the teachers made us gather round to talk tactics while we shivered. I always found it best to try to worm my way into the centre of the crowd of bodies, where there was, at least, a little warmth to be found.

This kind of treatment went against everything my mum believed in: keep yourself warm in winter, wrap a scarf round your neck, always wear a vest. But if I tried to keep a vest on under my shirt I'd be found out, jeered at, and made to take it back to the changing rooms. How I hated games lessons in winter. From the first whistle I'd be praying for them to be over, but time never seemed to speed like it did for more pleasant activities. If anything, it went more slowly! And then, when the awful ordeal was finally over, we would scoot back to the changing rooms where we had to face the showers!

Washing, to me, had always been something you did in private, with the bathroom door firmly locked, but now, it seemed, I was being asked to parade about stark naked with dozens of other boys. Towels had to be left outside the shower room, and once inside everyone tried desperately not to look at anyone else, all of us imagining, perhaps, that we were alone in the comfort of our own bathrooms, while we soaped away the mud. The only good thing about the showers, once you got over the obvious embarrassment, was that they warmed you up after the Arctic conditions outside. And yet, if you hadn't been quick enough, they'd turn cold before you'd washed away the mud, and you'd be left howling and jumping about while slapping yourself with icy water. Wrapping yourself in your towel was a real delight. But nobody ever had a chance to dry themselves properly. The masters would keep calling out to hurry up or the bus would leave without us, and we'd still be struggling to pull on socks over still-wet feet. Nobody fancied the three mile walk back to school, so we got a move on.

We did a lot of cross country running too. Occasionally they'd let us loose on the neighbourhood, but after one or two mishaps involving gates left open and cows wandering into cabbage fields, we were only allowed to run within the school grounds. Three laps were the minimum expected of new boys at the school. I stayed with the plodders at the back. Even though I could run fast, some of my friends couldn't, and it seemed unfriendly to zoom off into the distance and leave them behind. This often meant we were lapped by the really keen ones who finished the course before we'd even completed lap two. But I made sure I kept clear of the really slow lads, the ones who were carrying too much weight and were sadly jeered at by just about everyone, including the teachers, as they lumbered past the early finishers, with another lap still to go.

Sometimes the bell would sound for the end of the day and poor old Haynes or Watson would still be on their third lap, bent over at the far end of the field, puffing and winded, as the rest of us filed off to get changed. I imagined darkness falling and Watson crawling back on his hands and knees, only to find that everyone had left and his clothes were locked away in the changing room. Looking back on the way that Watson and others were treated, it seems dreadfully unfair, but back then no one seemed to think it wrong or damaging in any way. We always sympathised with Watson but were really glad that we weren't singled out for such treatment. The last thing you wanted at school was to stand out from the crowd.

CHAPTER TWENTY-TWO

Billy's Coming Back

The rumour spread round school like a fire spreads through a dry forest. Billy was coming back. It couldn't be true, it mustn't be true! We'd had nine months without him, nine months to lose the fear of him. Now it looked as if it would all be starting up once more. It seemed as if a black cloud was hanging over us all, and at any moment it would unleash a torrential downpour. It just wasn't fair.

Every day we expected to find him in the playground, expected to see his smirking face as he told us all how much he'd missed us. And one Monday he was there doing just that. He was back together with his old gang: Johnny Angel, Fingers Fletcher and Gerry the Ghoul. They were always round town at the weekend, too, and once again it wasn't safe to walk around on your own. There was a certain sort of safety in numbers, although even then it was still best to turn and run the moment we set eyes on him.

One afternoon we were at the beach, Paul, Richard, Andy and me. We had been rock pooling at Pegwell Bay, and were now returning to where we'd left our bikes. There were several big caves in the chalk cliffs of the bay, some of which we had explored, but there was one somewhat higher up in the cliffs than the others, and no one had yet managed to reach it.

What happened then was the result of a silly dare. Paul said it: 'I dare anyone to climb up to that cave.'

Stupidly, I'd always considered myself to be a bit of a mountain goat, and so I took up the challenge. There were places that I'd identified where I could find hand holds, and it looked as if my feet (which weren't too large) might rest on small ledges in the chalk. It was a climb of about four metres, I reckoned, and if I did fall, there was soft sand beneath that would cushion me. I might break and arm or a leg, but what was a dare without some element of danger?

I determined to take it very slowly and managed to reach about halfway without too much difficulty. My friends shouted encouragement from below. But we were all so engrossed in what I was doing that no one had seen Billy and his mates crossing the beach towards us.

The first thing we knew, he was calling out, 'Hey, look what we've got here. Target practice!'

He picked up a pebble and tossed it from hand to hand. I was terrified. There was nowhere I could go to escape. If I risked the drop to the Sands he'd be waiting there. If I carried on climbing, there would be a hail of missiles all around me. I pressed my body against the cliff face and offered up a swift prayer.

'Actually,' I heard him say, 'I've got a better idea. Let him climb up. Then once he's there, he's trapped. We'll hang about till the tide comes in. He can spend a night in the cave. That'll teach him a lesson.'

And the tide was rolling in. It had covered all the rock pools and was moving swiftly over the sand. Another hour or so and it would be lapping the base of the cliff. We knew about tides and tide tables. We needed to know these things living in a seaside town. There had been children cut off by the tide, some of whom had drowned. I knew I would be trapped, but it wouldn't be all night. My mates would tell their parents, tell mine too, and before long I'd be rescued. In some ways that was worse than bedding down for the night in the cave. I was sure to be in trouble for climbing up there in the first place.

Reluctantly I carried on climbing, with Billy and his gang calling me names and taunting me from below. I needed to concentrate, and it took a while before I was able to put one hand over the lip of the cave entrance and haul myself inside. Clapping and cheering broke out from my mates down below. The incoming sea was now much closer to the cliffs than before, and I was terribly worried.

The cave I'd climbed to was dark inside, but not too dark. As my eyes accustomed themselves to the gloom, I found that I could move around without too much difficulty. It looked as if the cave had been visited recently, as there were the charred remains of a fire near the entrance. There were also a couple of boxes and an old raincoat. I couldn't believe that someone had climbed the cliff while holding onto boxes.

That was when I started to think that maybe, just maybe, there might be another way into the cave. There was a glimmer of light near the back wall, and I went to investigate.

Down below on the beach I think everyone was starting to get bored. A few stones rattled into the cave behind me as I moved deeper inside. I started off along one wall, feeling to see if there were any breaks in the chalk that could offer me a way out, but it wasn't till I had gone as far towards the back as I could that I found some rough steps. They led upwards, further into the cliff. My heart was beating fast as I started to climb them. There would be a locked door at the top, I thought to myself, then I'd be no better off.

My mother used to say that we all had guardian angels looking after us. My angel was certainly holding my hand that day. The steps wound round and more light filtered through till finally I found bushes hiding what was obviously an alternative entrance. Unfortunately the bushes were mostly brambles, and I emerged onto the cliff top cut and scratched all over. It was still, I felt, a small price to pay for a fortunate escape. I sat there for a moment in the sunshine, thinking how lucky I'd been. What had saved me must have been one of the old smuggler's tunnels that had been used many years back to get stolen goods off of boats and into the country unnoticed.

I crawled to the cliff edge, where I could see what was happening down on the beach. Richard, Paul and Andy were edging away from Billy and his mates. I watched them turn and run towards where we'd left our bikes. Quickly I turned away and ran down to meet them. They stopped still, amazed to see me. Finger on my lips I signalled a silent getaway so that Billy and his gang would still think I was trapped in the cave. We pedalled furiously for a while and then threw down our bikes on the verge of the road and howled with laughter. We'd got one over on Billy for once.

On another occasion we ran into Billy and his gang when we were tadpoling on the marshes. It was less than ten minutes on the train to the marshes at Minster, where we could spend a pleasant day with jam jars and nets, scooping tadpoles out of the streams that criss-crossed the area. We would dip our nets again and again, pulling up weed, slime, mud and occasionally tadpoles that wriggled and slithered from net to jar.

We ate our sandwiches by the railway track, where we could watch the trains passing by and wave to the passengers inside. Then all at once Billy appeared with his mates trailing behind him, pushing and barging their way amongst us. Jars were carelessly knocked over, and the tadpoles were suddenly struggling to survive in the pools of water that spread around our feet.

Paul was furious and told Billy to leave us alone. Billy gave him a shove, and when Paul recovered, he came back at Billy with, 'Think you're hard then? I know something that you'd be frightened to do.'

'Nothing frightens me,' Billy sneered. 'Show me what it is.'

We walked for half a mile or so with Billy behind us making sure that we wouldn't run. He'd found some thin sticks of wood and was swishing them against the backs of our legs. Finally we found the place that Paul had in mind, where a sewer pipe crossed over a stream. It was about twenty centimetres in diameter and a distance of three metres or so from one bank to the other.

'I dare you,' Paul said to Billy, 'I dare you to walk along the pipe and not fall off.'

'I double dare you to do it first,' Billy came back at Paul.

Paul was good at gymnastics, and I knew he had a great sense of balance. He sat down and removed his shoes and socks before walking to the start of the pipe. He turned and looked at Billy. 'Shall we make it more of a challenge?'

'How?'

'Well, you only have thirty seconds to cross the stream.'

Billy was a large lad and really not as agile or adept as he believed himself to be, but he didn't want to lose face.

'OK.'

I don't think I could quite believe what happened next, and I'm certain that Billy didn't. Paul ran across the pipe. He didn't hesitate for one moment and was on the opposite bank in less than ten seconds. Looking back across the filthy water, he smiled at Billy. 'Your turn now.'

Billy, I'm sure, did not want to do what he'd been dared to do, but there was no way that he was going to back down. He moved towards the pipe.

'Don't you want to take off your shoes and socks?' Paul called. 'You'll get a better grip.'

Billy ignored him and placed both feet at the edge of the pipe. The shoes that he was wearing didn't look like they'd give him the best of grips, but he must have felt confident that they would. He set off taking big paces. Everything seemed OK and then… he wobbled, first one way and then the other. Then his foot slipped and down he crashed onto the pipe.

What Billy possessed between his legs, his manhood, his private parts, his tackle, took the full force of his weight. He let out a howl that must have been heard several miles away. Nearby, seagulls flew into the air, disturbed by the noise. Billy kept on howling and both my friends and Billy's gang were joined together at that moment in one shared feeling: we were really glad that wasn't us.

Then, as if matters couldn't get any worse for Billy, he tilted to the left, tried to regain his balance but slid from the pole in slow motion, hitting the water with a sizeable splash. It was very muddy and very smelly, but it wasn't very deep. Billy thrashed about for a bit trying to pull himself upright, but it must have been very slippery in all that mud, and he fell back down again. A second attempt didn't fare much better. It was obvious that Billy wouldn't make it out on his own. He needed the pulling power of others to release him from the mud's grasp.

'Let's not hang around for this,' I suggested, and we sped off, hoping to reach the station and catch a train back before Billy caught up with us. We debated whether he would be allowed on the train in such a wet and mud-covered state, but that wasn't our problem. What was our problem was Paul's parting shot as we ran off: 'Thanks for the entertainment, Billy.'

Today there would have been photographs of Billy's accident, captured on mobile phones, and a video on the Internet for everyone to laugh at, but in the early 1960s, all we had to help us was the power of our own description of the event. And we certainly did describe it – to everyone who wanted to listen.

It was tempting to think that this incident might end Billy's hold over us, and to some extent it did. But Billy's final humiliation was still to come.

Billy finally met his match in a girl called Beryl.

Beryl's younger brother, Derek, was constantly getting unwanted attention from Billy. Derek was small for his age, had a soft voice and easily burst into tears when something didn't go his way. Billy knew that Derek was an easy victim and had reduced him to tears on many occasions.

Billy waited for Derek each day and forced him to hand over his lunchbox. Billy would then take out most of what Derek's mum had given him, leaving him with just a packet of crisps. This went on for many weeks, and Derek could do nothing but just put up with it.

Then Billy started boasting that he enjoyed Derek's mum's sandwiches much more than the ones that his own mum gave him. Having had the misfortune to meet Billy's mum, I could quite understand that. I doubted there was much concern or attention as to what Billy was given for his lunch.

Derek, unfortunately, reached the point where he did not want to go to school. He'd pretend he had stomach ache to stay home. Beryl finally got out of him what the problem was. Normally Beryl and Derek kept out of each other's way and wouldn't dream of doing anything to help each other. But in families it is often said that 'blood is thicker than water', and Beryl didn't like to see someone outside the family upsetting her baby brother.

Beryl was the opposite of Derek. She was tall for her age and had a voice as loud as a foghorn. She had gathered a gang of girls around her who – like most of Ramsgate – had no time for Billy, and so together they hatched a plan.

One morning they followed Derek and watched from a distance as Billy investigated Derek's lunchbox. Then they raced towards Billy hollering and shrieking like banshees from Hell. Billy tried to run, but they surrounded him and tripped him up. Three of them sat on his chest while Beryl undid Billy's belt and pulled down his trousers.

Then they were off, waving their trophy trousers in the air as they headed towards the boys' school.

If I had been Billy at that point, I would have forgotten about rescuing my trousers and run home as fast as a cheetah on roller skates to find replacements. But Billy ran after his attackers with bare legs and shirt flapping around his middle.

In our school playground there was a flag pole where, on special occasions like the Queen's birthday or St George's Day, the flag would be raised. But today wasn't a special day – at least, not yet – and so the flag was missing. This suited Beryl's plan. She quickly tied Billy's trousers to the rope that raised the flag, pulled on the rope and hauled the trousers to the top of the pole, where they flapped around in the wind.

By this time there was the usual morning crowd of people in the playground and everyone turned to stare as a trouserless Billy burst through the school gate.

There were gasps of amazement, but, of course, nobody wanted to tell Billy that he'd forgotten an important piece of clothing in case Billy vented his anger on that person. However, one little lad, probably somebody's younger brother who hadn't yet started school, called out in a shrill voice, 'That boy isn't wearing any trousers!'

All at once everyone started pointing and laughing.

It was like a huge wave of laughter swelling and rolling its way around the playground. Billy stopped and stared around him, unable to believe that everyone's laughter was directed at him. He'd never been in such a situation before. 'Laughter' and 'Billy' were two words that just hadn't gone together up until now. He was puzzled. His brain was trying to come to terms with the fact that he, Big Billy, had somewhere along the line turned into an object of ridicule.

Then, those who were closest to Billy began to notice that there were yellow pee stains on his underpants.

My mum prided herself on the fact that I always had clean underwear each day. One of her greatest worries was that if I got knocked down by a car on my way to school, someone might find that I had dirty underwear. I failed to understand the logic in that. Surely underwear, whether dirty or clean, would be the last thing that anyone would be concerned about in a situation like that, but no. 'I wouldn't want someone undressing you in hospital,' she'd say, 'and finding out that you had dirty underwear. Whatever would they think?'

Billy's mum, however, must have had other views, for it looked as if Billy's pants hadn't been washed for weeks. Once, presumably, they must have been white, but now they were grey with yellow pee stains visible at the front.

For a second I almost felt sorry for Billy. Then I

remembered all the boys that Billy had upended and dunked head first in toilet bowls. He deserved all he got.

Beryl and her gang stepped back and Billy lifted his eyes to discover the whereabouts of his trousers. Just then, Mr Hardy appeared. In an instant he seemed to take in what was happening, and before we knew it, he was at the flag pole and pulling on the rope to lower the trousers. Wearily, with shoulders slumped and eyes downcast, Billy moved towards the flag pole, and when his trousers were within reach, he grabbed hold of them.

Tears were flowing freely now, and he wiped his eyes with the back of his hand, trying to stem the flow. He sat down, pulled off his shoes and heaved on his trousers. 'I think,' said Mr Hardy, looking at Beryl and her gang, 'that you girls need to get off to your own school now, or you'll be late.' And that was it. There was to be no telling off.

Then the school bell rang and we all began moving towards our classrooms. Somehow we knew that Billy had lost his power to terrify. He had, 'got his just desserts' – another of my mother's favourite sayings. I never understood that one. I thought 'desserts' were apple pie or jam sponge.

Later on my mother explained to me that what getting your just desserts really meant was that if you were a bad person and did bad things, sooner or later in your life someone would do bad things to you. That seemed to fit the situation, I thought. And Mr Hardy must have thought so too!

CHAPTER TWENTY-THREE

Awopbopaloobop

Getting in touch with someone is easy today. You can ring, text, email, message them on Facebook. But when I was a boy, the only way to arrange something with a friend was to go round his house and call for him. We did that all the time. 'Just going round Paul's,' I'd call to my mum. I spent a lot of time going round Paul's because his family had the first TV in our street. I was five or six years old and envious of Paul's luck. I'd gobble up my tea and then rush across the street to Paul's house, hoping I'd be invited in to watch *Robin Hood*, or westerns such as *Hopalong Cassidy*, *The Lone Ranger* or *The Cisco Kid*. These were heroes who rid the wild west of evil men whilst bending the law to their own ends. I'd sit with Paul's family in a darkened room, our eyes fixed on the flickering screen, while other kids knocked on Paul's door, hoping they'd be let in too.

My dad talked about maybe one day buying a TV, but that's all he did, just talk, and when I asked if we could have one, he'd say, 'Wait and see.'

Dad had been a 'wait and see' man all his life. It did me no good if I needled him or whined. 'Let's sleep on it,' he'd say, as if in the night some visitation would appear and give him a sign so next morning he'd know what to say. He needed working on by Mum. She knew how to get round him, to make him think it was his idea all along.

I was seven years old when Dad finally decided that he'd buy a television. It arrived in a wooden cabinet on legs and was set up in the corner of the room, where it could be plugged in. We all gathered round for the big switch on. To begin with nothing happened apart from a light coming on. 'We need to let it warm up,' Dad said, as a snowstorm picture appeared on the screen. Eventually the screen cleared and we watched our first television programme as a family. Quite often, as we were watching, the picture would dissolve into snowflakes once more, and Dad would have to adjust the aerial. The best picture seemed to come when Dad was standing on a chair with one arm holding the aerial aloft in what was a passable impression of the Statue of Liberty. Needless to say, it wasn't a position he could hold for very long.

If we needed to change the channel, there was no remote control. We had to get up from our seats and press a button on the television. Luckily, there wasn't much call for this, as for much of the time when I was growing up there were only two channels – BBC and ITV – until 1964, when BBC 2 started up. Programmes were only shown in the afternoon and evenings, and the stations closed down around 11.00pm. There was an hour of children's programmes between five and six o'clock each afternoon, and a show called *Watch with Mother* at lunchtime. This featured regular weekly spots with *Andy Pandy* – a hand puppet who lived in a nursery toy box – and *Bill and Ben, the Flower Pot Men* – two more puppets, who lived in flower pots, spoke to each other by repeating the words 'Flob-a-dob' and got excited about 'Little Weed' (who was actually a sunflower!). What really annoyed me though, to the extent that I would switch them off whenever they came on the TV, were a pair of singing pigs called Pinky and Perky. They 'sang' in high pitched voices that sounded like a record being rotated at twice the normal speed.

There were no video recorders or iPlayers, of course, and once a programme was shown, you couldn't see it again. If you missed a programme you had to rely on someone else to tell you what happened. Everything had to be fitted in around your favourite television serial. At 5.30pm on Saturday afternoons, the streets would be empty of kids as everyone was inside watching *Doctor Who*. (And although we wouldn't admit it, some of us were watching from behind the settee, especially when the Daleks appeared!)

One of my favourite programmes in the 1950s was a show for children called *Crackerjack*. Part of this programme was a quiz called 'Double or Drop'. In this three children had to answer general knowledge questions. When someone answered a question correctly, they were given prizes to hold. If a question was answered wrongly, a cabbage was added to the prizes. As more questions were answered it became increasingly difficult to hold onto the prizes without dropping something. If a contestant got two questions wrong or dropped an item, he or she was out. The winner was the child who managed to hold everything in place.

Daft really, but it had us hooked. We were all greedy and we all loved the idea of having armloads of prizes to take home.

A favourite cartoon programme was *Popeye the Sailorman*. Popeye's girlfriend was called Olive Oyl, and in each episode Popeye would have to rescue her from the unwanted attentions of a huge hulk called Bluto. Quite often Bluto would get the better of the weedy, outmatched Popeye and leave him lying on the floor, till Popeye, incensed at seeing Bluto running away with his girl, pulled out a can of spinach from inside his shirt. He'd swallow this in one gulp, and it would have the dramatic effect of transforming him into a musclebound hero capable of extraordinary feats of strength. He would then rescue Olive and defeat Bluto, all in the five minutes that it took to show this programme. The only downside was the infuriating theme song, which got into your brain and stayed there. My mates and I spent a lot of time making up rude versions of the song, which amused us all greatly at the time.

As they are today, television programmes on ITV were interrupted by adverts every ten or fifteen minutes. We often found these almost as entertaining as the programmes themselves. Again the advertisements would feature irritating jingles that lodged themselves in our brains, and we'd have great fun singing along. There was one that always seemed to be shown, featuring Heinz Baked Beans. A voice would sing, '*A million housewives everyday, pick up a tin of beans and say, Beanz Meanz Heinz*'.

In another, a voice would warble over a background of violins, '*You'll look a little lovelier each day, with fabulous pink Camay.*' Camay was a soap that smelled particularly pongy, at least in the opinion of small boys. I think we were all glad that the smell couldn't escape from the television. (Interesting point that – I wonder if anyone will every invent 'Smellyvision!')

But the worst of all was an advert, universally hated by my mates and I, that starred a very clean kitchen and glamorous mother who looked nothing like our stressed out mums. She would be pretending to do the washing up while a choir sang, '*Now hands that do dishes can feel soft as your face with mild green Fairy Liquid.*' Ugh, we thought, a thousand times ugh! But no matter how annoying the advert, the fact that I had a TV at all was enough to make up for it.

Until we had our own TV, all my entertainment had come from the radio.

Lunchtimes, when I was young, it was *Listen with Mother*. And we did listen, my mum and I, while the voice in the radio asked, 'Are you sitting comfortably? Then I'll begin...'

Then, every Saturday morning, there was 'Uncle Mac', who played an hour or two of the type of music that the BBC thought children would like to hear and ought to hear. There were story songs, such as the one about the three Billy goats gruff and the troll that lived under the bridge. The goats all wanted to eat the lush grass in the field on the other side of the bridge, while the troll beneath it threatened to eat them if they tried to cross it. '*Fol de roll, I'm a troll,*' he'd sing as they came near.

Then there was *The Runaway Train,* about the little engine that struggled to haul his carriages up a hill, with the words, '*I think I can, I think I can...*'

There was Sparky's Magic Piano, Nellie the Elephant who packed her bags and said goodbye to the circus, and a song called *76 Trombones*, which was about a parade of instrument players. One line always made me laugh: '*...with a big bang bong... from a big bang bonger at the rear.*'

Other favourites were *How Much is That Doggie in the Window?*, *Me and My Teddy Bear*, *I Taut I Taw a Puddy Tat* (*I Thought I Saw a Pussy Cat*), *The Laughing Policeman* and the one about an emperor who paraded down the street without his clothes on. Some dodgy tailors had convinced the Emperor that they'd made him a wonderful suit of clothes that only intelligent and clever people could see. The Emperor didn't want to admit that he couldn't see the clothes for fear of looking an idiot, and everyone watching felt the same. So they praised the Emperor's new suit until one small boy who hadn't heard about the Emperor's new clothes shouted out to everyone that he was 'altogether as naked as the day that he was born!' That always amused me.

Another good one was *There Was an Old Lady Who Swallowed a Fly*. This started out as you might expect. But then to catch the fly, the old lady had to swallow a spider, a bird to catch the spider, a cat to catch the bird, a dog to catch the cat, a goat to catch the dog, a cow to catch the goat, and finally a horse, at which point, she died!

There was also a track by a comedian called Tommy Cooper with the wonderful title, *Daddy, Don't Jump off the Roof*, and another by Charlie Drake called *My Boomerang Won't Come Back* (It wasn't actually faulty. He sang about dropping it and waving it around but failed to realise that a boomerang will only come back if you throw it!). A song called *The Laughing Policeman* was actually somebody laughing for most of the record, and as laughter is infectious, it always got me laughing too

But my absolute number one favourite tune was a love song about two toothbrushes. I think its title was, *You're a Pink Toothbrush, I'm a Blue Toothbrush*, and it was sung with great sincerity by Max Bygraves. It had such classic lines as:

> *You're a pink toothbrush, I'm a blue toothbrush,*
> *won't you marry me in haste.*
> *I'll be true toothbrush, just to you toothbrush,*
> *if we both use the same toothpaste.*

Another song by Max Bygraves had the wonderful title of *Gilly-Gilly Ossenfeffer Katzenellen Bogen by the Sea*. What that meant, nobody seemed to know.

Later I got into Lonnie Donegan, who recorded such

wonderful songs as *Does Your Chewing Gum Lose its Flavour on the Bedpost Overnight?* and the brilliant *My Old Man's a Dustman*. This contained lines that always made me laugh, such as when the dustman is chased after by a lady whose bin he has skipped. She says, 'You've missed me, am I too late?', and he replies, 'No, jump up on the cart.' Loved it then, still do.

Soon after this I started listening to *Radio Luxembourg*. This was a European music station broadcasting from the tiny country of Luxembourg, and the disc jockeys (DJs) who played the records called it 'Your Station of the Stars'.

The reception was poor, more buzz and crackles than music, but occasionally, when everything seemed to be working OK (and the wind was blowing in the right direction!) I would hear snatches of rock 'n' roll: Elvis Presley singing '*You ain't nothing but a hound dog*' or Little Richard screeching out a song with the most amazing first line: '*Awopbopaloobopalopbamboom*'. This was from a song called *Tutti Frutti*. Don't ask me what it all meant, but it sounded fabulous. Google it one day.

I had a tiny radio to listen on, a transistor radio – or 'trannie' as it was known – and when my mother had said goodnight and gone downstairs, I'd reach out for the radio, turn it on softly and hide it under the covers.

At the same time, I started listening to my father's records, which I played on his wind up gramophone. The record would spin and the music play, and I would sit back, close my eyes and let the sounds wash over me. That is, until the gramophone began to slow down, in need of another wind. Then I realised something that kept me entertained for hours: that a record developed a certain *something* when rotated at different speeds. My favourite recording to mess around with was *Stranger in Paradise* by Tony Bennett. I would let his voice slow down to a soupy growl then furiously wind the handle to speed it up again. Tony's voice would increase in pitch until it sounded like he was wearing a pair of the tightest trousers ever made! As you can imagine, my father disapproved of my treating his prize records in such a way, but that never stopped me.

Then I began to enjoy a British rock 'n' roller called Cliff Richard. You might know him these days as that old bloke off the telly, but both he and his backing group, The Shadows, were pretty cool at the start of the 1960s. The lead guitarist of The Shadows was a tall, thin guy who wore thick rimmed glasses. His name was Hank Marvin and every boy who ever strummed a guitar wanted to play like Hank.

Sunday afternoons there was *Pick of the Pops* with a DJ called Alan 'Fluff' Freeman. I never did understand what the 'Fluff' stood for, but his show was a rundown of the ten top-selling records for that week. At the beginning of every programme, he'd welcome us all with 'Greetings, Pop Pickers.' It became a show I never missed, taking my 'trannie' with me wherever I went so that I could tune in. It was 1962 and I was twelve. Music was becoming more important to me by the day.

About this time my cousin David (the expert swimmer and diver) came to live with us. He was seventeen and sadly had lost both of his parents at a young age. Dave brought his motorbike, which really impressed me, although my mum wouldn't let me ride on it, and some great records which I was able to borrow and play on my record player. This was my introduction to Buddy Holly, a rock and roll singer who died in a plane crash in 1959. I loved his songs then and still do today.

Later that year I heard The Beatles for the first time. *Love Me Do* was a simple enough song, but the combination of hoarse vocals, electric guitars and wailing harmonica instantly had me hooked. But who was producing this wonderful noise? *The New Musical Express* filled me in on the details. Four lads from Liverpool: John Lennon (the raw voice on 'Love Me Do'), Paul McCartney, George Harrison and Ringo Starr. From their photographs I could see that they had long hair, not the normal short back and sides cut that everybody seemed to have those days.

When their second record appeared in 1963, it stormed up the charts to number two, and I was able to see The Beatles on television for the first time. Dad didn't approve. 'They need a haircut,' he announced. Records

were six shillings and eightpence, (about thirty-three p.)
David bought a copy and we played it again and again.
He bought their first album too, the day it was released,
and I was the envy of my friends because I could listen
to it.

One day Dad brought home a tape recorder that he'd
picked up second hand in a junk shop, and this opened
up a whole world of new opportunities. I could now tape
what I heard playing on the radio and listen to it again.
Unfortunately I could only use a microphone to tape the
songs, and this had to be placed close to the radio speaker.
Even then what was taped was often fuzzy and at a much
lower volume. The microphone would also pick up
sounds from around the room, and in quieter passages
all sorts of things could be heard: the budgie's chirping
or Chum's barking, even, on one occasion, my mum
asking if I needed the toilet! But who cared if the quality
was poor, or if the disc jockey spoke over the
introduction. I could now listen to my favourite music
again and again and again.

These days, when it's possible to hear any music track
you want to at the click of a mouse, it's strange to
remember how the only way I could hear my favourite
track was to wait by the radio in the hope that it would
be played at some point in the day.

In March 1964 a ship on the North Sea began
broadcasting pop music to Britain. This was *Radio*

Caroline. It was unlicensed to broadcast, and according to the government, this was illegal. But it was an 'all day music station', as the DJs told us, broadcasting from 6.00am to 6.00pm. For those of us who loved music, it was heaven. I could listen non-stop to The Beatles, The Rolling Stones, The Kinks, The Animals, The Who and the American singer/songwriter Bob Dylan.

The first time I heard Bob Dylan's song *The Times They Are a-Changin'*, my mind, as they used to say in the Sixties, was well and truly blown. The first thing to hit me was the voice, well, lack of voice anyway. But more than anything, what really connected with me were the words that he sang:

Come mothers and fathers throughout the land,
your sons and your daughters are beyond your command...

He understood how I was feeling, like my mum and dad didn't. He understood those first stirrings of rebellion in a teenage kid who wanted to rebel but wasn't brave enough. He understood me, a geeky little boy from England, and was saying what I had been feeling and what I hadn't been able to put into words...

My parents bought me a guitar. It was an acoustic guitar and not the flashy red Stratocaster that I really wanted. The neck was quite thick at the top and it was difficult to get my fingers around it to form chords. I loved the whole idea of being able to play the guitar and I practiced till my finger tips began to get sore. I didn't make much progress either, just about mastered the simplest three chords but stringing them together and then singing over the top was a real problem.

I stood for ages in front of the mirror, striking all kinds of poses with my guitar. I loved the idea of being a pop star, but even the thought that I might one day serenade Sally wasn't enough to keep me focused. I tried writing one or two songs but they were hopeless. I put the guitar away but carried on writing. What I wrote next was poetry of a sort. I filled notebooks with ideas and lines and lengthy poems that rambled on for page after page.

My parents wondered what I was doing, shut away in my room for hours at a time. Finally I confessed, showed them one or two poems that I hoped might impress them.

Later my dad knocked on my door, came into my room and stood there for a moment till I stopped writing and turned to look at him. He cleared his throat as if about to make some momentous statement. Finally he said, 'It's good that you've got a hobby, but you mustn't neglect your school work.' He turned to leave and then added, 'Writing poems is OK but it'll never earn you a living.'

He was right about lots of things, but wrong about that one as I've earned a living from poetry for nearly thirty years now! But if you really want to know how I became a poet, well that's another story.

BRIAN MOSES

'One of Britain's favourite children's poets.' The Poetry Archive

Brian Moses lives in the Sussex village of Burwash with his wife Anne, and a loopy Labrador called Honey. (The writer Rudyard Kipling once lived in Burwash in a somewhat larger house than Brian's.)

He first worked as a teacher but has now been a professional children's poet since 1988. To date he has over 200 books published including volumes of his own poetry such as *A Cat Called Elvis* and *Behind the Staffroom Door* (both Macmillan), anthologies such as *The Secret Lives of Teachers* and *Aliens Stole My Underpants* (both Macmillan) and picture books such as *Beetle in the Bathroom* and *Trouble at the Dinosaur Cafe* (both Puffin). He also co-wrote *What Are We Fighting For? – New Poems About War* with children's poet Roger Stevens.

Over 1 million copies of Brian's poetry books have now been sold by Macmillan.

Brian also visits schools to run writing workshops and perform his own poetry and percussion shows. To date he has visited well over 2500 schools and libraries throughout the UK and abroad. At the request of Prince Charles he spoke at the Prince's Summer School for Teachers in 2007 at Cambridge University and *CBBC* commissioned him to write a poem for the Queen's 80th birthday. He is featured on the Poetry Archive – poetry archive.org/brianmoses

Visit Brian's website: brianmoses.co.uk
and his blog: brian-moses.blogspot.com

Also available from Candy Jar Books

TOMMY PARKER: Destiny Will Find You
by Anthony Ormond

When Tommy Parker packs his bag and goes to his grandpa's house for the summer he has no idea that his life is about to change forever.

But that's exactly what happens when his grandpa lets him in on a fantastic secret. He has a pen that lets him travel through his own memories and alter the past. Imagine that! Being able to travel into your own past and re-write your future.

Tommy Parker: Destiny Will Find You! is an exhilarating adventure that redefines the time travel genre.

You'll never look at your memories in quite the same way again...

ISBN: 978-0-9928607-1-4